Current
CONTROVERSIES

Interference in Elections

Other Books in the Current Controversies Series

Current
CONTROVERSIES

Interference in Elections

Kristina Lyn Heitkamp, Book Editor

GREENHAVEN
PUBLISHING

Published in 2019 by Greenhaven Publishing, LLC
353 3rd Avenue, Suite 255, New York, NY 10010

Copyright © 2019 by Greenhaven Publishing, LLC

First Edition

Cover image: Alexandru Nika/Shutterstock.com

Library of Congress Cataloging-in-Publication Data

Names: Heitkamp, Kristina Lyn, editor.
Title: Interference in elections / Kristina Lyn Heitkamp, book editor.
Description: New York : Greenhaven Publishing, [2019] | Series: Current
  controversies | Includes bibliographical references and index. | Audience: Grades 9–12.
Identifiers: LCCN 2018028334| ISBN 9781534503878 (library bound) | ISBN
  9781534504615 (pbk.)
Subjects: LCSH: Elections—Corrupt practices—United States. | Electronic
  voting—Security measures—United States. | Presidents—United
  States—Election, 2016. | Hacking—Russia (Federation)
Classification: LCC JK1994 .I67 2018 | DDC 324.973/0932—dc23
LC record available at https://lccn.loc.gov/2018028334

Manufactured in the United States of America

Website: http://greenhavenpublishing.com

Contents

Chapter 1: Should We Replace Voting Machines with Paper Ballots?

Brian Barrett

The United States' electronic voting system is in desperate need of a massive update. Interference in elections points to the vulnerabilities and insecurities of electronic voting machines.

Yes: Paper Ballots Are Reliable and Secure

Taylor Armerding

The electronic voting machines used around the country are antiquated and insecure and are at risk of crashing, which could lead to lost votes.

Timothy B. Lee

A bipartisan group of six senators heed the advice of computer scientists that paperless electronic voting machines are vulnerable to hacking and can't be meaningfully audited. The new legislation would help eliminate paperless machines.

Vanessa Teague

Australia's election procedures involve using paper ballots to vote and then automating the results, making the process of counting votes easier and more efficient while enabling the vote to be audited by counting paper ballots. If a glitch or potential interference occurs, it is possible to check the results against the physical ballots.

Robert Mueller's indictment against Russia's Internet Research Agency proves that its meddling was more than just a simple ruse. The Russian effort was sophisticated, planned, and well funded.

No: Russian Officials Deny Interference

Chapter 3: Are Social Media and Fake News Responsible for 2016 Election Interference?

Yes: Social Media Plays a Powerful Part in Many Voter's Lives

No: Social Media Is Not to Blame for Interference

Foreword

"Controversy" is a word that has an undeniably unpleasant connotation. It carries a definite negative charge. Controversy can spoil family gatherings, spread a chill around classroom and campus discussion, inflame public discourse, open raw civic wounds, and lead to the ouster of public officials. We often feel that controversy is almost akin to bad manners, a rude and shocking eruption of that which must not be spoken or thought of in polite, tightly guarded society. To avoid controversy, to quell controversy, is often seen as a public good, a victory for etiquette, perhaps even a moral or ethical imperative.

Yet the studious, deliberate avoidance of controversy is also a whitewashing, a denial, a death threat to democracy. It is a false sterilizing and sanitizing and superficial ordering of the messy, ragged, chaotic, at times ugly processes by which a healthy democracy identifies and confronts challenges, engages in passionate debate about appropriate approaches and solutions, and arrives at something like a consensus and a broadly accepted and supported way forward. Controversy is the megaphone, the speaker's corner, the public square through which the citizenry finds and uses its voice. Controversy is the life's blood of our democracy and absolutely essential to the vibrant health of our society.

Our present age is certainly no stranger to controversy. We are consumed by fierce debates about technology, privacy, political correctness, poverty, violence, crime and policing, guns, immigration, civil and human rights, terrorism, militarism, environmental protection, and gender and racial equality. Loudly competing voices are raised every day, shouting opposing opinions, putting forth competing agendas, and summoning starkly different visions of a utopian or dystopian future. Often these voices attempt to shout the others down; there is precious little listening and considering among the cacophonous din. Yet listening and considering, too, are essential to the health of a democracy. If controversy is democracy's lusty lifeblood, respectful listening and careful thought are its higher faculties, its brain, its conscience.

Current Controversies does not shy away from or attempt to hush the loudly competing voices. It seeks to provide readers with as wide and representative as possible a range of articulate voices on any given controversy of the day, separates each one out to allow it to be heard clearly and fairly, and encourages careful listening to each of these well-crafted, thoughtfully expressed opinions, supplied by some of today's leading academics, thinkers, analysts, politicians, policy makers, economists, activists, change agents, and advocates. Only after listening to a wide range of opinions on an issue, evaluating the strengths and weaknesses of each argument, assessing how well the facts and available evidence mesh with the stated opinions and conclusions, and thoughtfully and critically examining one's own beliefs and conscience can the reader begin to arrive at his or her own conclusions and articulate his or her own stance on the spotlighted controversy.

This process is facilitated and supported in each Current Controversies volume by an introduction and chapter overviews that provide readers with the essential context they need to begin engaging with the spotlighted controversies, with the debates surrounding them, and with their own perhaps shifting or nascent opinions on them. Chapters are organized around several key questions that are answered with diverse opinions representing all points on the political spectrum. In its content, organization, and methodology, readers are encouraged to determine the authors' point of view and purpose, interrogate and analyze the various arguments and their rhetoric and structure, evaluate the arguments' strengths and weaknesses, test their claims against available facts and evidence, judge the validity of the reasoning, and bring into clearer, sharper focus the reader's own beliefs and conclusions and how they may differ from or align with those in the collection or those of classmates.

Research has shown that reading comprehension skills improve dramatically when students are provided with compelling, intriguing, and relevant "discussable" texts. The subject matter of these collections could not be more compelling, intriguing, or urgently relevant to today's students and the world they are poised to inherit. The anthologized articles also provide the basis for stimulating, lively, and passionate classroom debates. Students who are compelled to anticipate objections to their own argument and identify the flaws in those of an opponent read more carefully, think more critically, and steep themselves in relevant context, facts, and information more thoroughly. In short, using discussable text of the kind provided by every single volume in the Current Controversies series encourages close reading, facilitates reading comprehension, fosters research, strengthens critical thinking, and greatly enlivens and energizes classroom discussion and participation. The entire learning process is deepened, extended, and strengthened.

If we are to foster a knowledgeable, responsible, active, and engaged citizenry, we must provide readers with the intellectual, interpretive, and critical-thinking tools and experience necessary to make sense of the world around them and of the all-important debates and arguments that inform it. We must encourage them not to run away from or attempt to quell controversy but to embrace it in a responsible, conscientious, and thoughtful way, to sharpen and strengthen their own informed opinions by listening to and critically analyzing those of others. This series encourages respectful engagement with and analysis of current controversies and competing opinions and fosters a resulting increase in the strength and rigor of one's own opinions and stances. As such, it helps readers assume their rightful place in the public square and provides them with the skills necessary to uphold their awesome responsibility—guaranteeing the continued and future health of a vital, vibrant, and free democracy.

Introduction

> *"Voting is completely important.*
> *People in America think democracy*
> *is a given. I think of it as an*
> *ecosystem, and what gets in the way*
> *of it is politicians and apathy. What's*
> *amazing is, so many people, and*
> *they're not bad people, they just don't*
> *do it. Now, more than ever, I would*
> *hope that people would be lining up*
> *and frothing at the mouth."[1]*
>
> *— Henry Rollins*

One of the most important rights of American citizens is the right to vote. The right to cast a vote is the foundation of what defines our nation's democracy. However in the early history of voting a considerable percentage of the population was denied a voice in American truth and justice. Voting was largely a privilege reserved for white men who owned property. The path to voting rights for all American citizens was a long and arduous fight: women suffragettes were jailed and brutally force-fed while on a hunger strike.[2] Forty activists courageously died fighting for minority voting rights during the modern Civil Rights Movement, including Dr. Martin Luther King Jr.[3]

Voting is fundamental to the equality of all Americans. Citizens, regardless of race, gender, religion, or social economic status, deserve a government determined by and working for its entire population. And when a mainstay of justice is disrupted, it sours the integrity of the country. Since the Russian interference in the

US 2016 presidential election, policymakers and voters have been left scratching their heads, wondering how our election system could have been hacked and if the interference in our election had any serious consequences.

Some election officials claim it is a mechanical issue and that we need to get back to basics and use paper ballots again. Both cost-effective and reliable, paper ballots cannot be hacked and leave a trail that can be audited. But others suggest that we need to exit the Stone Age and get with the e-voting times. They counter that the real error lies in human hands with paper ballots.

While some argue whether we should be able to cast a vote from the comfort of our couch, others claim that concerns about inference reach far beyond the ballot box. Government officials are wondering how and where the modern world meets elections. Social media and online fake news were prevalent problems in the 2016 US presidential election and will likely continue to be issues. Misinformation campaigns will persevere to overtake many threads of democratic discourse. But who is ultimately responsible? The finger pointing has gone around the table many times. A controversial conversation, some believe social media companies should be held accountable for providing an easy podium for invaders to spew rhetoric and prompt discord, while others say we should blame the manipulator, not the messenger.

Although election interference is a problem, some argue that is not a new one. Indeed, Russia is not the only country with a reputation for election interference—the *New York Times* highlighted that the United States has been doing it for years. Loch K. Johnson, political science professor and author of several books on foreign affairs, has investigated the long history of the United States meddling in other countries' elections. "We've been doing this kind of thing since the CIA was created in 1947... We've used posters, pamphlets, mailers, banners — you name it. We've planted false information in foreign newspapers. We've used what the British call 'King George's cavalry': suitcases of cash," Johnson said.[4] Although Johnson admits the US has been playing the game, he also says that the intent in these situations was different. In the past, the CIA meddled as a way to combat immoral leaders.

Whether the intent is to fight injustice or influence the vote and insert chaos in political discourse, experts argue about the appropriate consequences for interfering with the United States' election process. National security expert Adam Segal believes that sanctioning Russia is just one step among many that needs to be taken to ensure a well-functioning democracy:

> The responses fall in three boxes. First, there is the calling out of the Russians, punishing them for previous attacks, and deterring them for future ones. The recent Mueller indictments are a step in the right direction. While the Russians mentioned in the indictment will never see a US court, the United States is demonstrating to Russia, and others, that it can attribute the interference and hopefully make them think longer about whether it is useful to launch future attempts.[5]

Regardless of which mask it wears, inference in elections is an issue that will likely resurface every election cycle and attempt to obfuscate the integrity of voting. The viewpoints in *Current Controversies: Interference in Elections* explore the different roles found in America's election ecosystem, including voters, social media companies, and government officials. Computer scientists weigh in on the security of our current electronic voting system. A political analyst investigates why Russia was successful this time around, while a historian grapples with America's own history of interference. The different perspectives will help readers navigate the political game and may engender deeper appreciation for the right to vote. As notable former President Abraham Lincoln asserted, "Elections belong to the people. It's their decision. If they decide to turn their back on the fire and burn their behinds, then they will just have to sit on their blisters."[6]

Notes

1. Beth Winegarner, "3-minute interview with Henry Rollins," *The Examiner*, November 5, 2007. https://archives.sfexaminer.com/sanfrancisco/3-minute-interview-with-henry-rollins/Content?oid=2149400

2. Doris Stevens, *Jailed for Freedom*, Boni and Liveright, 1920.

3. Southern Poverty Law Center, "History: Civil Rights Memorial," Retrieved June 1, 2018. https://www.splcenter.org/what-we-do/civil-rights-memorial/history

4. Scott Shane, "Russia Isn't the Only One Meddling in Elections. We Do It, Too," *New York Times*, Feb. 17, 2018. https://www.nytimes.com/2018/02/17/sunday-review/russia-isnt-the-only-one-meddling-in-elections-we-do-it-too.html

5. Emily Stewart, "Russian election interference is far from over. I asked 9 experts how to stop it," *Vox,* February 19, 2018. https://www.vox.com/policy-and-politics/2018/2/19/17023240/election-2018-russia-interference-stop-prevent

6. Ben Epstein, *The Only Constant is Change*, Oxford University Press, 2018.

CHAPTER 1

Should We Replace Voting Machines with Paper Ballots?

America's Electronic Voting Systems Are Easy Targets

Brian Barrett

Brian Barrett is a news editor with WIRED.

T his week, GOP presidential candidate Donald Trump openly speculated that this election would be "rigged." Last month, Russia decided to take an active role in our election. There's no basis for questioning the results of a vote that's still months away. But the interference and aspersions do merit a fresh look at the woeful state of our outdated, insecure electronic voting machines.

We've previously discussed the sad state of electronic voting machines in America, but it's worth a closer look as we approach election day itself, and within the context of increased cyber-hostilities between the US and Russia. Besides, by now states have had plenty of warning since a damning report by the Brennan Center for Justice about our voting machine vulnerabilities came out last September. Surely matters must have improved since then.

Well, not exactly. In fact, not really at all.

Rise of the Machines

Most people remember the vote-counting debacle of the 2000 election, the dangling chads that resulted in the Supreme Court breaking a Bush-Gore deadlock. What people may not remember is the resulting Help America Vote Act (HAVA), passed in 2002, which among other objectives worked to phase out the use of the punchcard voting systems that had caused millions of ballots to be tossed.

In many cases, those dated machines were replaced with electronic voting systems. The intentions were pure. The consequences were a technological train wreck.

"America's Electronic Voting Machines Are Scarily Easy Targets," by Brian Barrett, Condé Nast, August 2, 2016. Reprinted by permission.

"People weren't thinking about voting system security or all the additional challenges that come with electronic voting systems," says the Brennan Center's Lawrence Norden. "Moving to electronic voting systems solved a lot of problems, but created a lot of new ones."

The list of those problems is what you'd expect from any computer or, more specifically, any computer that's a decade or older. Most of these machines are running Windows XP, for which Microsoft hasn't released a security patch since April 2014. Though there's no evidence of direct voting machine interference to date, researchers have demonstrated that many of them are susceptible to malware or, equally if not more alarming, a well-timed denial of service attack.

"When people think that people think about doing something major to impact our election results at the voting machine, they think they'd try to switch results," says Norden, referring to potential software tampering. "But you can do a lot less than that and do a lot of damage… If you have machines not working, or working slowly, that could create lots of problems too, preventing people from voting at all."

The extent of vulnerability isn't just hypothetical; late last summer, Virginia decertified thousands of insecure WinVote machines. As one security researcher described it, "anyone within a half mile could have modified every vote, undetected" without "any technical expertise." The vendor had gone out of business years prior.

The WinVote systems are an extreme case, but not an isolated one. Other voting machine models have potentially vulnerable wireless components; Virginia's just the only one where a test proved how bad the situation was.

The worst part about the current state of voting machines is that they don't even require outside interference to undo an election. "They're all computers. They run on tens of thousands of lines of code," says Norden. "It's impossible to have a perfectly secure, perfectly reliable computer."

That's true, but in fairness, most computers aren't quite this imperfect, either.

A Good Kind of Audit

So electronic voting machines aren't ideal. The good news is, it's entirely possible to mitigate any potential harm they might cause, either by malice or mistake.

First, it's important to realize that electronic voting machines aren't as commonplace as one might assume. Three-quarters of the country will vote on a paper ballot this fall, says Pamela Smith, president of Verified Voting, a group that promotes best practices at the polls. Only five states—Delaware, Georgia, Louisiana, South Carolina, and New Jersey—use "direct recording electronic" (DRE) machines exclusively. But lots of other states use electronic machines in some capacity. Verified Voting also has a handy map of who votes using what equipment, which lets you drill down both to specific counties and machine brands, so you can see what's in use at your polling station.

More than half of the states conduct post-election auditing, by checking vote totals against paper records, to ensure that the votes are accurate. Both Smith and Norden agree that this sort of auditing is the single best way to guarantee confidence in election results, as does MIT computer scientist Ronald Rivest, who has written extensively on voting machine issues.

The problem is that not every state does post-election audits. And even some that require them by law, namely Pennsylvania and Kentucky, don't actually use voter-verifiable paper trails, meaning they have no way to complete an audit. And progress toward more and better auditing is slow; Maryland just put an auditable system in place this year, Smith says, and will pilot it during the fall election. Over a dozen states still have no audit procedure at all.

The problem with putting these auditing systems in place is the same one keeping more reliable voting machines from the booths in the first place: a lack of money and political will. There's new voting equipment out there that's much more secure than the machines states purchased in bulk a decade or more ago, but only a handful of states and municipalities—Rhode Island, DC, and parts of Wisconsin among them—have upgraded in the past year.

"The money's not there right now," says Norden. "We interviewed election officials who told us what they were hearing from their state legislators and others who would be funding this type of equipment, and they say come back to us after there's some kind of crisis."

Which, if they wait long enough, is exactly what they're going to get.

Rigging the Vote

For what it's worth, electronic voting machines have been this hackable in previous elections as well, and there's no indication—even in Virginia—that there's ever been any interference.

This year feels different though, in no small measure because of Russia's alleged responsibility for the DNC hack. If Putin would go so far as release those emails, would he pursue a direct assault on our vulnerable voting machines as well?

The short answer? Nyet.

"Putin's not very nice, but he's not stupid," says Ryan Maness, a visiting fellow at Northeastern University who specializes in international cyber conflict and Russian foreign policy. "If they were going to mess with the voting machines and the vote-counting software, they wouldn't have done the DNC hack."

Maness argues that the DNC hack and subsequent email release has put a spotlight on Russia. The blowback from such direct interference in a United States election would be too severe. Besides, Maness says, Putin's main objective was likely to embarrass Hillary Clinton, rather than elevate Trump. And he's certainly achieved that much already.

But even if Maness is wrong, the even better news is that the three states that will likely decide the election—Florida, Ohio, and Pennsylvania—have voting machines that are in relatively good shape. Florida has an audit requirement in place, while Ohio not only conducts audits, Smith says, it has an "automatic recount provision," where close races trigger a manual recount without requiring a candidate to request one. "Pennsylvania is of the most concern" among those three, says Smith, "based on the fact they have so many paperless DREs in use." Even there, though, election officials will actively deploy paper ballots in the event that those machines fail.

Still, unlikelihood that Russia would tamper with our voting machines hasn't lifted the sense of unease around the election. When Donald Trump suggests the election might be "rigged," he's referring to a host of potential disruptions, from the times and dates of scheduled debates to whatever else he might bend to his narrative. In November, should he lose, he'll find the voting machines to be an easy target.

That suspicion is the real danger of electronic voting systems, and especially of those that can't be easily or effectively audited. If you can't guarantee that there was no tampering—which not every state can—it might not matter if any actually took place. In the wrong hands, the doubt itself is damaging enough.

Paper Is the Quick and Easy Fix for Hackable Voting Machines

Taylor Armerding

Taylor Armerding is an award-winning journalist who has been writing in the IT security field for the past six years. Previously he wrote for CSO Online.

Want better security of election voting results? Use paper. With the US almost halfway between the last national election and the 2018 mid-terms, not nearly enough has been done yet to improve the demonstrated insecurity of current electronic voting systems. Multiple experts say one obvious, fundamental move should be to ensure there is a paper trail for every vote.

That was a major recommendation at a panel discussion this past week that included representatives of the hacker conference DefCon and the Atlantic Council think tank, which concluded that while there is progress, it is slow.

The progress includes the designation of voting systems as critical infrastructure by the Department of Homeland Security, plus moves in Texas and Virginia to improve the security of their systems by using paper.

Most states already do that. But Lawrence Norden, co-author of a September 2015 report for the Brennan Center for Justice titled "America's Voting Machines at Risk," wrote in a blog post last May for The Atlantic that 14 states, "including some jurisdictions in Georgia, Pennsylvania, Virginia, and Texas – still use paperless electronic voting machines. These systems should be replaced as soon as possible."

There is little debate about the porous nature of electronic voting systems – it has been reported for years. It was close to

"The fix is in for hackable voting machines: use paper," by Taylor Armerding, Sophos Ltd., October 17, 2017. Reprinted by permission.

four years ago, in January 2014 that the bipartisan Presidential Commission on Election Administration (PCEA) declared:

> *There is an impending crisis ... from the widespread wearing out of voting machines purchased a decade ago. ... Jurisdictions do not have the money to purchase new machines, and legal and market constraints prevent the development of machines they would want even if they had funds.*

A couple of years later the Brennan Center issued its report, which predicted that in the 2016 elections, 43 states would be using electronic voting machines that were at least 10 years old – "perilously close to the end of most systems' expected lifespan."

The biggest risk from that, the report said, was failures and crashes, which could lead to long lines at voting locations and lost votes. But it also said security risks were at unacceptable levels:

> *Virginia recently decertified a voting system used in 24 percent of precincts after finding that an external party could access the machine's wireless features to "record voting data or inject malicious data.*
>
> *Smaller problems can also shake public confidence. Several election officials mentioned "flipped votes" on touch screen machines, where a voter touches the name of one candidate, but the machine registers it as a selection for another.*

Not to mention that with solely digital voting machines, there is no way to audit the results.

While there is still no documented evidence that hostile nation states – mainly Russia – have been able to tamper directly with election results, the risk is there. At this past summer's DefCon conference, one of the most high-profile events was the so-called Voting Village, where Wired reported that, "hundreds of hackers got to physically interact with – and compromise – actual US voting machines for the first time ever."

The reason it hadn't been done before, at least publicly, was that it was illegal. But at the end of 2016, an exemption to the

Digital Millennium Copyright Act finally legalized hacking of voting machines for research purposes.

Not surprisingly, hackers didn't have all that much trouble – they found multiple ways to breach the systems both physically and with remote access. And according to Jake Braun, a DefCon Voting Village organizer and University of Chicago researcher, the results undermined the claim that the decentralized voting system in the US (there are more than 8,000 jurisdictions in the 50 states) would make it more difficult to hack.

With only a handful of companies manufacturing electronic voting machines, a single compromised supply chain could impact elections across multiple states at once, he noted.

It's not just tampering with actual voting results that can damage the credibility of an election either. Norden told Wired that, "you can do a lot less than that and do a lot of damage… If you have machines not working, or working slowly, that could create lots of problems too, preventing people from voting at all."

Norden doesn't dismiss the need for technology improvements. "Among the wide variety of solutions being explored or proposed are use of encryption, blockchain, and open source software," he wrote in his blog post.

But the most effective security measure, he contended in his blog post, is low-tech:

> *The most important technology for enhancing security has been around for millennia: paper. Specifically, every new voting machine in the United States should have a paper record that the voter reviews, and that can be used later to check the electronic totals that are reported.*
>
> *This could be a paper ballot the voter fills out before it is scanned by a machine, or a record created by the machine on which the voter makes her selections—so long as she can review that record and make changes before casting her vote.*

That kind of improvement doesn't have to take a lot of time or cost big bucks either, he said, and would create, "software independent" voting systems, where an, "undetected change or error in its software cannot cause an undetectable change or error in an election outcome."

Given what are sure to be continued attempts at foreign interference in US elections, "it is the least we can do," he said.

Government Officials Attempt to Secure Future Elections with Paper

Timothy B. Lee

Timothy B. Lee holds a master's degree in computer science from Princeton. He has written for the Washington Post *and Vox. He covers technology policy, blockchain technologies, and the future of transportation.*

A bipartisan group of six senators has introduced legislation that would take a huge step toward securing elections in the United States. Called the Secure Elections Act, the bill aims to eliminate insecure paperless voting machines from American elections while promoting routine audits that would dramatically reduce the danger of interference from foreign governments.

The legislation comes on the heels of the contentious 2016 election. Post-election investigation hasn't turned up any evidence that foreign governments actually altered any votes. However, we do know that Russians were probing American voting systems ahead of the 2016 election, laying groundwork for what could have become a direct attack on American democracy.

"With the 2018 elections just around the corner, Russia will be back to interfere again," said co-sponsor Sen. Kamala Harris (D-Calif.).

So a group of senators led by James Lankford (R-Okla.) wants to shore up the security of American voting systems ahead of the 2018 and 2020 elections. And the senators have focused on two major changes that have broad support from voting security experts.

The first objective is to get rid of paperless electronic voting machines. Computer scientists have been warning for more than a decade that these machines are vulnerable to hacking and can't be meaningfully audited. States have begun moving away from

"New bill could finally get rid of paperless voting machines," by Timothy B. Lee, Condé Nast, January 2, 2018. Reprinted by permission.

paperless systems, but budget constraints have forced some to continue relying on insecure paperless equipment. The Secure Elections Act would give states grants specifically earmarked for replacing these systems with more secure systems that use voter-verified paper ballots.

The legislation's second big idea is to encourage states to perform routine post-election audits based on modern statistical techniques. Many states today only conduct recounts in the event of very close election outcomes. And these recounts involve counting a fixed percentage of ballots. That often leads to either counting way too many ballots (wasting taxpayer money) or too few (failing to fully verify the election outcome).

The Lankford bill would encourage states to adopt more statistically sophisticated procedures to count as many ballots as needed to verify an election result was correct—and no more.

We talked to two election security experts who praised the legislation and urged Congress to pass it quickly.

"We're rapidly running out of time," says Lawrence Norden, an election expert at the Brennan Center at New York University Law School. Given the long lead times involved in planning for a major election, he told us, Congress will have to move quickly if it wants new recommendations to be ready before the 2018 election—or new voting systems to be in place by November 2020.

The Bill Would Drive a Stake through the Heart of Paperless Voting

America's approach to elections has changed dramatically since 2000, when butterfly ballots and hanging chads threw a presidential election into chaos. In 2002, Congress appropriated billions of dollars to help states replace outdated voting systems.

Unfortunately, much of this money was used to buy paperless touchscreen voting machines. These seemed like the wave of the future, but computer security experts found them to be seriously inadequate.

"Computer scientists were worried about them from the start," according to Alex Halderman, a computer scientist at the

University of Michigan. They worried "that they were being rolled out too fast and without effective security standards."

"In every single case, when a machine was brought into the lab and studied by qualified researchers, the result was the discovery of significant vulnerabilities that could allow the machines to be compromised with malicious software that could potentially steal votes," Halderman told Ars.

So Halderman says that, over the last decade, "the thinking has shifted to looking at more practical solutions." In particular, election security experts have come to regard optical-scanned paper ballots as the gold standard for computer security.

Optical-scan ballots can be counted by machine to provide prompt and accurate vote totals. But if there's any doubt about the integrity of the results, there's always an option to do a hand recount of the paper ballots.

The Lankford bill would enshrine this thinking into federal law. "Funds received under a grant under this section may not be used for any voting system that records each vote in electronic storage unless the system is an optical scanner that reads paper ballots," the bill says.

That approach makes sense to Norden, too. "The paperless systems are probably the least secure systems and also among the oldest systems in the country," he told Ars.

The legislation sets up a nationwide process to identify these machines and phase them out. States wanting money would need to submit a list of current machines that don't use paper ballots and a plan for replacing those machines. The states would then get grant money that could only be used for replacing those machines.

Mindful of state prerogatives over election administration, the bill doesn't go as far as banning the use of paperless machines. States would be free to continue using them if they wanted to. But the legislation would give state election administrators a powerful shove toward better voting systems—and it's likely that many states would take the hint and the money.

Post-Election Audits Would Become
Routine and Statistically Rigorous

The problem with the way many states currently handle post-election audits is illustrated by last fall's controversy over recounts in the key swing states of Wisconsin, Pennsylvania, and Michigan. Liberal activists and some election security experts wanted recounts to make sure that the close and surprising results in those states were legitimate. But the move angered Republicans who felt that the recount drive was simply an effort to cast doubt on the legitimacy of the election result.

At the same time, the statewide recounts were expensive. Green Party presidential candidate Dr. Jill Stein raised $3.5 million to fund a statewide recount in Wisconsin that turned up no signs of irregularities. Counting every ballot in the state was probably overkill given that Trump won with a small but comfortable margin of 20,000 votes.

Halderman argues that a better approach would be to make a post-vote audit a routine step in the election process. When every election is followed by an audit, it removes the potential stigma and controversy that came with the 2016 recounts.

Some states already do post-election audits, but even here Halderman argues there›s room for improvements. States can maximize the effectiveness of these audits and minimize costs by varying the size of each recount based on the victory margin.

"When the public policy space was less sophisticated about statistics, lawmakers picked a fraction of precincts or auditing units to examine—one percent or something like that," Halderman told Ars. "But, over the past decade, the statistical science about election auditing has really blossomed."

"You want to treat the process of auditing an election as a process of gathering evidence that the election result was right," Halderman says. "You start examining ballots and you stop after you've gathered enough evidence to convince yourself at a defined level of certainty."

"An audit isn't necessarily a recount if an election result is not particularly close," Halderman says. "You don't have to look at that many ballots in order to audit it to high confidence. But if an election result turns on one vote, obviously you do need to look at every ballot to know that for sure."

Obviously, this is more expensive than having no post-election checks. But it could be a lot less expensive than a rule that requires auditing a fixed fraction of all ballots after every election.

More important, the statistical rigor of these recounts would provide a powerful deterrent to anyone thinking about tampering with American elections, since the probability of tampering going undetected would be very low.

Rather than mandating a specific auditing procedure, the bill creates an advisory committee that would be heavily staffed by election security experts. These experts would be tasked with developing a set of standards for robust election auditing. States could then apply for money to implement improvements to their election procedures that are consistent with these expert recommendations.

One concern about a process for variable-size recounts is that it can make the costs of conducting an election unpredictable. If an election is particularly close, it can require counting all of the ballots to have a high confidence that the result was correct. And that could create a financial crunch for election officials with fixed budgets.

To address that concern, the Lankford bill creates an insurance pool to reimburse states when close elections force them to do wide-ranging recounts.

"I Think It's Very Positive"

The Lankford bill has other important provisions, too. It would take several steps to encourage more information sharing between state and federal officials about suspected attacks. The bill would require voting equipment vendors to promptly notify the relevant authorities about cybersecurity incidents. It would help state election officials to get security clearances so they can receive classified briefings from intelligence agencies.

But Lawrence Norden, the elections expert from New York University, argues that the most important thing about the bill is who's sponsoring it. The bill has three Republican co-sponsors and three Democrats, giving it bipartisan appeal. And as the press release for the legislation notes, co-sponsors Lankford and Harris are the "only members of the Senate who serve on both the Homeland Security Committee and Intelligence Committee"—which Norden says is important for a bill that's related to national security.

"In terms of what the bill does, I think it's very positive," Norden told Ars. "It checks off the boxes for what needs to be done."

But Norden stressed that it's important for Congress to move quickly if it wants to have an impact on the 2018 election—or even give election officials time to fully prepare for the 2020 election.

The legislation establishes an expert panel and gives it 180 days to set guidelines for election security. If those guidelines are going to have any impact on the 2018 election, Congress needs to pass the bill as soon as possible, Norden argues.

Indeed, there's little time to waste even for the 2020 election, according to Norden. The legislation envisions states drawing up plans to replace outdated election systems and institute new voting procedures, then applying for federal funding to implement those plans. Once the federal funding is approved, states will then have to purchase the equipment, set it up, train election officials, and so forth. That could easily take the bulk of the time between now and November 2020.

Paper Audits Are Necessary for Secure Automated Vote Counting

Vanessa Teague

Vanessa Teague is a senior lecturer in the department of computing and information systems at the University of Melbourne. Her main research interest is electronic voting, with a focus on cryptographic schemes for end-to-end verifiable elections.

Australia's paper-based elections have built up trust over generations through the deployment of carefully considered processes. The most crucial of these is candidate-appointed scrutineering. The ability to observe and scrutinise the process provides critical protection against errors and malfeasance.

The Senate count is partially automated, which is a good thing, but the evidence of its accuracy must be able to be checked by human scrutineers. This is more important than ever because the new Senate voting rules mean handwritten preferences will make a difference.

We agree "it is essential that a random sample of the paper Senate ballots be checked against the final published electronic votes used for counting".

Computers Don't Remove the Need for Scrutiny

Election software in Australia has had procedural errors, software bugs and security problems that have affected running systems and (probabilistically) at least one election outcome. (Physical ballot security is also important of course.)

The NSW Electoral Commission recently released PwC's report into the 2015 iVote internet voting project. iVote input 280,000 votes into the state election tally. Voters could vote from

"Paper Audits Crucial for Automated Counting," by Dr. Vanessa Teague, Pursuit at the University of Melbourne, August 2, 2016. This article was first published in Pursuit. Read the original article at https://pursuit.unimelb.edu.au/articles/paper-audits-crucial-for-automated-counting#. Licensed under CC BY-ND 3.0 AU.

home or from a polling place over the internet. Since meaningful candidate-appointed scrutineering was impossible, the auditing task was entrusted to PwC. Their report was released last month after a delay of more than a year – it is now too late for any unsuccessful candidate to appeal the accuracy of the outcome.

PwC observed a series of testing and certification processes, culminating in a "lockdown" of the software prior to the election run, which they summarise: "Review of the lockdown process ... Prior to live voting NSWEC (New South Wales Electoral Commission) were required to secure iVote to prevent unauthorised access to the system, as this could invalidate or impact the integrity of the voting process."

There are a number of concerning aspects of the report:

1. There was an unplanned software update two weeks into early polling, the day before election day: "PwC was present on 27/03/2015 to observe the unlocking of the system, due to a change that was required" and "Lockdown was removed for Scytl to make performance improvements to the CVS database".

2. The CVS database is the Core Voting System database, the equivalent of an electronic ballot box holding all the iVotes. An update to that database is the electronic equivalent of undoing the seals on that ballot box and rearranging the ballots, an action we would not expect a contractor to perform on paper ballots except under careful observation by scrutineers.

3. We have argued elsewhere that private certification and testing is no substitute for public scrutiny. We learn now that even that process was bypassed. We don't see how that unplanned software update could possibly have been subjected to a rigorous testing and certification process while the system was running. And if the software had been thoroughly tested and certified in advance, why did it need to be updated?

4. Even more concerning is a one-line remark about the verification process, "Fix signature file, which was preventing verification". So how many verifications did the un-fixed signature file prevent? When was it fixed?

5. Perhaps the strangest thing about PwC's report is that it doesn't say, of all those people who tried to verify their vote, what fraction failed.

How to Scrutinise the Senate Count

The lesson for the Senate count is clear: the integrity of the election result must depend, not on the perfect security and accuracy of the software, but on Australian scrutineers watching a careful audit of the paper evidence of how Australians voted.

So how can we do that?

The preferences will be manually entered in parallel with the automated digitising system, and scrutineers will be able to compare a digital image of the ballot with the interpreted preferences displayed on the screen. This might be a good way of checking for accidental scanning errors or character recognition problems. However, if there's a software bug, database problem, procedural error, or security breach, those numbers that the scrutineers see on the screen might not match the paper votes or the final output.

There are two quite separate steps: A digitising step, in which the paper ballots are converted in to an electronic list of preferences, and a counting step, in which those preferences are turned into a list of winning senators.

The counting step is easy to check: download one of the open source Senate vote counting applications available online and recount the published preferences for yourself. Of course, that code too might be buggy, but at least you can read it or reimplement your own. (The official code is a trade secret, despite the Senate itself having passed a motion requesting its publication.)

The digitising step is also easy to check: the Australian Electoral Commission should, in the presence of scrutineers, perform a rigorous random audit of the paper evidence to check that it matches the preference data file. Some ideas:

- Choose a reasonable sample size and do an audit. This at least gives us an estimate of the error rate.
- Perform a Bayesian Audit to see if any small samples of the paper ballots produce a different election outcome. Perhaps extend this by looking at individual ballots and keeping track of discrepancies between the data file and the paper.
- Try to compute a bound on the number of errors that could change the election outcome, then use a Risk Limiting Audit against that possibility.

We could have several teams each doing a different analysis of the same audit data.

Conclusion

Scrutineers must have a chance to verify that the election outcome was right. A simple statistical audit of the paper evidence will greatly lower the chance that bugs or security problems give us an unnoticed wrong Senate outcome.

Blame How Data Is Processed, Not the Machines

Steve Ragan

Prior to joining the journalism world in 2005, Steve Ragan spent fifteen years as a freelance IT contractor focused on infrastructure management and security.

Every time there's an election, the topic of hacking one comes to the surface. During a presidential election, that conversation gets louder. Yet, even the elections held every two years see some sort of vote hacking coverage. But can you really hack an election? Maybe, but that depends on your goals.

The topic of election hacking is different this year, and that's because someone is actually hacking political targets. Adding fuel to the fire, on Aug. 12, 2016, during an event in Pennsylvania, Donald Trump warned the crowd that if he loses the battleground state, it's because the vote was rigged.

"The only way we can lose, in my opinion — and I really mean this, Pennsylvania — is if cheating goes on," Trump said. This was no random remark either, Pennsylvania voting has been called in to question before. Such was the case when Republican supporters claimed Mitt Romney lost the state in 2008 due to fraud.

When it comes to hacking elections, most people imagine voting machines compromised in such a way that a vote for candidate 'A' actually counts as a vote for candidate 'B' – or the votes just disappear.

However, security experts who have tackled the topic of election hacking often come to a single conclusion, while the machines that process votes are riddled with vulnerabilities – 278 disclosed historically, none with a CVE ID assignment – they're not the problem. The real attack surface is the way voters are processed.

"Hacking an election is about influence and disruption, not voting machines," by Steve Ragan, CSO, October 5, 2016. Reprinted by permission.

In a recent Privacy XChange Forum survey including 2,004 people, nearly 40 percent of those questioned said they were concerned about the amount of personal data in the possession of political parties and campaigns.

Earlier this year, CSO Online's Salted Hash, working alongside researcher Chris Vickery, broke the news that 191 million voter records were exposed due to database configuration issues.

All of the information in the two databases came from the political parties, local election boards, and the voters themselves – who submitted it as part of a focused Q&A, donation questionnaire, or the data was collected from data brokers and public records.

Records like the ones exposed earlier this year are collected, sorted, sold, and shared among political operatives and campaigns; yet, every single record started out as a basic voter registration form.

This is where the problem, and the reality of hacking an election, begins to unfold.

Target the Systems Running the Vote

"The biggest obstacle for hackers seeking to rig the vote count is the lack of standardization for electronic voting mechanisms across states, which may have very different systems," said Rook Security's Security Operations Leader, Mat Gangwer.

"The decentralization of a common voting standard contains the damage if attackers were to compromise a particular system. In order to be successful enough to influence a national election, hackers must carefully select where and what to attack. At a macro level, hackers only need to focus on the handful of battleground states that are likely to influence the winner."

Another key element would be the need to focus on areas that lack an auditable trail of paper ballots and large population centers that could conceivably "experience" a swing in votes large enough to matter at the state level. An election with high-expected voter turnout would also serve as cover.

A sad fact, referenced by the FBI, is that the election process is secured by obscurity. It's so "clunky and dispersed" that hacking the infrastructure directly makes the task of hacking an election nearly impossible.

Target the Campaigns Directly

"It is no small feat to steal an election but, it is not beyond the realm of possibility," said Dave Lewis, security advocate for Akamai, and CSO Online blogger.

No matter what, he added, the effort would require a prolonged campaign to collect information on their target.

"The attackers would probe the defenses of the other party looking for any low-hanging fruit such as poorly secured systems. Once the homework has been done, they will attempt to comprise systems listed from their research," Lewis said.

"The goal here will be to collect as much information as they can gather from the other campaign such as campaign strategies, voter lists, emails. The point here is to be able to counter the moves of the opposite candidate on the political stage. Knowing the game plan in advance would not hurt for the attackers. As well, being able to leak internal communications can be used in an attempt to discredit the target candidate."

In addition to all of that, the attackers would also need to run a focused social media campaign to help sway public opinion.

"We have seen that sort of activity in the current US election as well as in the elections of other countries," Lewis added.

Polling data can also be a source of influence as a means to compromise an election.

"If I were a hacker, I wouldn't hack the voting systems. I'd wait until the data were aggregated from the polls and then hack that data. Leading up to the elections a lot of attention is on polls - if the data on the polls can be manipulated or lost, it would create chaos in the campaigns and reduce trust in the final election outcome," said Amol Kabe, vice president of product management at Netskope.

Soft Targets

As mentioned, the topic of election hacking is usually only discussed during election season, but this year is different, because someone is actually hacking political targets, including Hilary Clinton and voter registration databases.

In August, someone leaked an Amber TLP memo from the FBI, this was unusual because advisories such as this rarely go public.

The leaked memo cites details released by MS-ISAC (Multi-State Information Sharing Analysis Center), stating that foreign actors are using common scanning tools to locate and compromise vulnerable election systems in Illinois and Arizona. Salted Hash covered the memo at length, including all of the technical details released by MS-ISAC and the FBI.

Recently, reports of two additional voter registration system compromises have started to circulate online. However, these rumors are only supported by anonymous sources cited by ABC News. One of the suspected states, Florida, denied that there were any problems.

On September 28 FBI Director James Comey told the House Judiciary Committee "there's no doubt that some bad actors have been poking around" on voter registration systems.

"There have been a variety of scanning activities, which is a preamble for potential intrusion activities as well as some attempted intrusions at voter registration databases beyond those we knew about in July and August. We are urging the states just to make sure that their deadbolts are thrown and their locks are on, and to get the best information they can from DHS just to make sure their systems are secure," Comey said in response to questions.

"And again, these are the voter registration systems. This is very different than the vote system in the United States, which is very, very hard for someone to hack into because it's so clunky and dispersed – it's Marry and Fred putting a machine under the basketball hoop at the gym. Those things are not connected to the internet, but the voter registration systems are."

Twenty-four hours earlier, on Sept. 27, Jeh C. Johnson, Secretary of the U.S. Department of Homeland Security, told the

Senate Committee on Homeland Security and Governmental Affairs, his agency has reached out with offers of assistance to state and election officials.

The DHS offer includes remotely conducted cyber hygiene scans on internet-facing systems; on-site risk and vulnerability assessments; access to the NCCIC 24x7 incident response center; sharing of relevant information on cyber incidents and best practices; and access to field-based cybersecurity and protective security advisers.

"...to date, 18 states have requested our assistance," Johnson said.

It's important to remember that the registration databases in Arizona and Illinois were targeted and compromised via common tools and methods. The attackers, whoever they were, didn't need to be advanced or highly skilled, they just needed to know how to click a button and download results.

Moreover, the DHS protection is basic, focusing on best practices and a checklist mentality for security – something experts disagree with, because attack surfaces are unique and can change from network to network.

It's About Influence, Not Voting Machines

In an interview with CSO Online, Carson Sweet, CTO of CloudPassage, mirrored Lewis' and Gangwer's opinions – influencing the outcome of the voting process by compromising voting machines is improbable, but not impossible.

"We're not on the brink of democracy's digital implosion, but we have a lot of work left to do. In any case, it's about much more than just the voting machines, so let's not get myopic and lose track of the bigger picture," Sweet said.

According to ballotpedia.org, most of the voting technology used these days is either mostly paper-based or uses a paper backup to direct recording electronic (DRE) systems.

About 14 percent of electoral votes are in swing states where some percentage of voting machines are DRE without a paper backup – specifically Florida, Virginia, and Pennsylvania. But even in those cases, some districts use paper ballots and DRE with paper backups. Only one state, Louisiana, uses DRE with no paper backup at all.

"This means that irregularities in vote counts, either by compromising the voting machine or election management software (the "back-end" to voting machines) would be recognized in spot-checks or manual verification counts, which many states still perform," Sweet said.

"Keep in mind that just compromising a few machines is not enough, unless you could see into the future to know exactly where those extra 500 votes would matter. You would have to compromise enough machines to guarantee a win; otherwise, what's the point?"

Sweet says that if he were to construct a scenario in which he could impact a vote, the approach would be to disrupt voting in the swing states and other key voting areas.

So how would he do this?

"By compromising online voter databases well before the election," he explains.

"Federal law requiring that voter records be unified online actually make this easier for an attacker since there's only one place to go per state (e.g. California's VoteCal system)," Sweet added.

Imagine what would happen if an attacker were able to dissociate physical signatures from voter records. Or perhaps the attacker could randomly scramble the last six digits of someone's Social Security number; mark a significant number of voters as deceased - or some combination of all of the above.

If done too broadly, Sweet explained, it would cause pandemonium at a voting site. Yet, if done with just the right amount and with consistency, the blame might likely land on bad administration or voters who incorrectly registered.

"By invalidating the ability for my opponent's voters to cast their ballots, I could significantly and broadly disrupt voting and their overall voting count," Sweet said.

"I mean let's face it, have *you* logged in to verify that all your voter registration data is correct?"

The Issues with Electronic Voting Machines Are Fixable

Bruce Schneier

Bruce Schneier is an internationally renowned security technologist. He is the author of thirteen books as well as hundreds of articles, essays, and academic papers.

In the aftermath of the U.S.'s 2004 election, electronic voting machines are again in the news. Computerized machines lost votes, subtracted votes instead of adding them, and doubled votes. Because many of these machines have no paper audit trails, a large number of votes will never be counted. And while it is unlikely that deliberate voting-machine fraud changed the result of the presidential election, the Internet is buzzing with rumors and allegations of fraud in a number of different jurisdictions and races. It is still too early to tell if any of these problems affected any individual elections. Over the next several weeks we'll see whether any of the information crystallizes into something significant.

The U.S has been here before. After 2000, voting machine problems made international headlines. The government appropriated money to fix the problems nationwide. Unfortunately, electronic voting machines — although presented as the solution — have largely made the problem worse. This doesn't mean that these machines should be abandoned, but they need to be designed to increase both their accuracy, and peoples' trust in their accuracy. This is difficult, but not impossible.

Before I can discuss electronic voting machines, I need to explain why voting is so difficult. Basically, a voting system has four required characteristics:

"The Problem with Electronic Voting Machines," by Bruce Schneier, November 9, 2004. Reprinted by permission. https://www.schneier.com/blog/archives/2004/11/the_problem_wit.html

1. Accuracy. The goal of any voting system is to establish the intent of each individual voter, and translate those intents into a final tally. To the extent that a voting system fails to do this, it is undesirable. This characteristic also includes security: It should be impossible to change someone else's vote, ballot stuff, destroy votes, or otherwise affect the accuracy of the final tally.

2. Anonymity. Secret ballots are fundamental to democracy, and voting systems must be designed to facilitate voter anonymity.

3. Scalability. Voting systems need to be able to handle very large elections. One hundred million people vote for president in the United States. About 372 million people voted in India's June elections, and over 115 million in Brazil's October elections. The complexity of an election is another issue. Unlike many countries where the national election is a single vote for a person or a party, a United States voter is faced with dozens of individual election: national, local, and everything in between.

4. Speed. Voting systems should produce results quickly. This is particularly important in the United States, where people expect to learn the results of the day's election before bedtime. It's less important in other countries, where people don't mind waiting days — or even weeks — before the winner is announced.

Through the centuries, different technologies have done their best. Stones and pot shards dropped in Greek vases gave way to paper ballots dropped in sealed boxes. Mechanical voting booths, punch cards, and then optical scan machines replaced hand-counted ballots. New computerized voting machines promise even more efficiency, and Internet voting even more convenience.

But in the rush to improve speed and scalability, accuracy has been sacrificed. And to reiterate: accuracy is not how well the ballots are counted by, for example, a punch-card reader. It's not how the tabulating machine deals with hanging chads, pregnant chads, or anything like that. Accuracy is how well the process translates voter intent into properly counted votes.

Technologies get in the way of accuracy by adding steps. Each additional step means more potential errors, simply because no technology is perfect. Consider an optical-scan voting system. The voter fills in ovals on a piece of paper, which is fed into an optical-scan reader. The reader senses the filled-in ovals and tabulates the votes. This system has several steps: voter to ballot to ovals to optical reader to vote tabulator to centralized total.

At each step, errors can occur. If the ballot is confusing, then some voters will fill in the wrong ovals. If a voter doesn't fill them in properly, or if the reader is malfunctioning, then the sensor won't sense the ovals properly. Mistakes in tabulation — either in the machine or when machine totals get aggregated into larger totals — also cause errors. A manual system — tallying the ballots by hand, and then doing it again to double-check — is more accurate simply because there are fewer steps.

The error rates in modern systems can be significant. Some voting technologies have a 5% error rate: one in twenty people who vote using the system don't have their votes counted properly. This system works anyway because most of the time errors don't matter. If you assume that the errors are uniformly distributed — in other words, that they affect each candidate with equal probability — then they won't affect the final outcome except in very close races. So we're willing to sacrifice accuracy to get a voting system that will more quickly handle large and complicated elections. In close races, errors can affect the outcome, and that's the point of a recount. A recount is an alternate system of tabulating votes: one that is slower (because it's manual), simpler (because it just focuses on one race), and therefore more accurate.

Note that this is only true if everyone votes using the same machines. If parts of town that tend to support candidate A use a voting system with a higher error rate than the voting system used in parts of town that tend to support candidate B, then the results will be skewed against candidate A. This is an important consideration in voting accuracy, although tangential to the topic of this essay.

With this background, the issue of computerized voting machines becomes clear. Actually, "computerized voting machines" is a bad choice of words. Many of today's voting technologies involve computers. Computers tabulate both punch-card and optical-scan machines. The current debate centers around all-computer voting systems, primarily touch-screen systems, called Direct Record Electronic (DRE) machines. (The voting system used in India's most recent election — a computer with a series of buttons — is subject to the same issues.) In these systems the voter is presented with a list of choices on a screen, perhaps multiple screens if there are multiple elections, and he indicates his choice by touching the screen. These machines are easy to use, produce final tallies immediately after the polls close, and can handle very complicated elections. They also can display instructions in different languages and allow for the blind or otherwise handicapped to vote without assistance.

They're also more error-prone. The very same software that makes touch-screen voting systems so friendly also makes them inaccurate. And even worse, they're inaccurate in precisely the worst possible way.

Bugs in software are commonplace, as any computer user knows. Computer programs regularly malfunction, sometimes in surprising and subtle ways. This is true for all software, including the software in computerized voting machines. For example:

In Fairfax County, VA, in 2003, a programming error in the electronic voting machines caused them to mysteriously subtract 100 votes from one particular candidates' totals.

In San Bernardino County, CA in 2001, a programming error caused the computer to look for votes in the wrong portion of the ballot in 33 local elections, which meant that no votes registered on those ballots for that election. A recount was done by hand.

In Volusia County, FL in 2000, an electronic voting machine gave Al Gore a final vote count of negative 16,022 votes.

The 2003 election in Boone County, IA, had the electronic vote-counting equipment showing that more than 140,000 votes had been cast in the Nov. 4 municipal elections. The county has only 50,000 residents and less than half of them were eligible to vote in this election.

There are literally hundreds of similar stories.

What's important about these problems is not that they resulted in a less accurate tally, but that the errors were not uniformly distributed; they affected one candidate more than the other. This means that you can't assume that errors will cancel each other out and not affect the election; you have to assume that any error will skew the results significantly.

Another issue is that software can be hacked. That is, someone can deliberately introduce an error that modifies the result in favor of his preferred candidate. This has nothing to do with whether the voting machines are hooked up to the Internet on election day. The threat is that the computer code could be modified while it is being developed and tested, either by one of the programmers or a hacker who gains access to the voting machine company's network. It's much easier to surreptitiously modify a software system than a hardware system, and it's much easier to make these modifications undetectable.

A third issue is that these problems can have further-reaching effects in software. A problem with a manual machine just affects that machine. A software problem, whether accidental or intentional, can affect many thousands of machines — and skew the results of an entire election.

Some have argued in favor of touch-screen voting systems, citing the millions of dollars that are handled every day by ATMs and other computerized financial systems. That argument ignores another vital characteristic of voting systems: anonymity. Computerized financial systems get most of their security from audit. If a problem is suspected, auditors can go back through the records of the system and figure out what happened. And if the problem turns out to be real, the transaction can be unwound and fixed. Because elections are anonymous, that kind of security just isn't possible.

None of this means that we should abandon touch-screen voting; the benefits of DRE machines are too great to throw away. But it does mean that we need to recognize its limitations, and design systems that can be accurate despite them.

Computer security experts are unanimous on what to do. (Some voting experts disagree, but I think we're all much better off listening to the computer security experts. The problems here are with the computer, not with the fact that the computer is being used in a voting application.) And they have two recommendations:

1. DRE machines must have a voter-verifiable paper audit trails (sometimes called a voter-verified paper ballot). This is a paper ballot printed out by the voting machine, which the voter is allowed to look at and verify. He doesn't take it home with him. Either he looks at it on the machine behind a glass screen, or he takes the paper and puts it into a ballot box. The point of this is twofold. One, it allows the voter to confirm that his vote was recorded in the manner he intended. And two, it provides the mechanism for a recount if there are problems with the machine.

2. Software used on DRE machines must be open to public scrutiny. This also has two functions. One, it allows any interested party to examine the software and find bugs, which can then be corrected. This public analysis improves security. And two, it increases public confidence in the voting process. If the software is public, no one can insinuate that the voting system has unfairness built into the code. (Companies that make these machines regularly argue that they need to keep their software secret for security reasons. Don't believe them. In this instance, secrecy has nothing to do with security.)

Computerized systems with these characteristics won't be perfect — no piece of software is — but they'll be much better than what we have now. We need to start treating voting software like we treat any other high-reliability system. The auditing that is conducted on slot machine software in the U.S. is significantly more meticulous than what is done to voting software. The development process for mission-critical airplane software makes voting software look like a slapdash affair. If we care about the integrity of our elections, this has to change.

Proponents of DREs often point to successful elections as "proof" that the systems work. That completely misses the point. The fear is that errors in the software — either accidental or deliberately introduced — can undetectably alter the final tallies. An election without any detected problems is no more a proof the system is reliable and secure than a night that no one broke into your house is proof that your door locks work. Maybe no one tried, or maybe someone tried and succeeded...and you don't know it.

Even if we get the technology right, we still won't be done. If the goal of a voting system is to accurately translate voter intent into a final tally, the voting machine is only one part of the overall system. In the 2004 U.S. election, problems with voter registration, untrained poll workers, ballot design, and procedures for handling problems resulted in far more votes not being counted than problems with the technology. But if we're going to spend money on new voting technology, it makes sense to spend it on technology that makes the problem easier instead of harder.

Voting Machines Were Not Hacked, But Voters Were Attacked

Richard Forno

Richard Forno is a senior lecturer in the University of Maryland, Baltimore County department of computer science and electrical engineering, where he directs the UMBC Graduate Cybersecurity Program and serves as the Assistant Director of UMBC's Center for Cybersecurity.

The presidential campaign of 2016 thankfully – and we can only hope officially – ended this evening. As of when this article was posted, there are no reports of widespread cyberattacks or other digital interference against state voting systems. Of course, since votes are still being tallied, we're not in the clear yet. But current indications are that this was a fairly uneventful election, from a cybersecurity perspective at least.

So far, we've seen no public evidence of Russian hackers, 400-pound or otherwise, attacking individual voting machines from their bedrooms (to use a very tired old trope). There have been reports of brief computer problems, but they were easily remedied. And there's no indication that state voter registration databases were compromised by hostile third parties.

Nevertheless, cybersecurity units of several states' National Guard forces were mobilized ahead of the election, in a manner reminiscent of the reassuring and public show of force when airports reopened following 9/11. The military's hackers at U.S. Cyber Command reportedly stood ready to retaliate against cyberattacks on the election – in particular, from Russia as well.

These possibilities and preparations reinforce the need for America to place a greater emphasis on election-related

"This election was not hacked – but it was attacked," by Richard Forno, The Conversation, November 9, 2016. https://theconversation.com/this-election-was-not-hacked-but-it-was-attacked-67511. Licensed Under CC BY-ND 4.0 International.

cybersecurity, if not also cybersecurity more generally. Even though nothing suspicious appears to suggest the election was "hacked," we must still make improvements. At stake is the trustworthiness of the electoral systems and processes of the world's leading democracy.

Time for Governments to Act

Politically motivated digital attacks during the latter months of election 2016 raised concerns about the electronic security of the American electoral process. These events included the hacking of the Democratic National Committee and the ongoing Wikileaks disclosures of email accounts of Clinton advisers. These events increased public interest in cybersecurity beyond the effects of the revelations of NSA contractor Edward Snowden in 2013 and many high-profile data breaches.

In recent months, government agencies and experts (including myself) have recommended improvements to the electronic security of our hodgepodge collection of voting systems.

Among our suggestions are that states ensure their voting systems are modernized, properly updated, tested and secured from both physical and network-based tampering. States must continually ensure the integrity of their voter databases to help minimize the potential for voter fraud. And they must provide a trusted audit trail (for example, paper receipts) for election officials and the public to fall back on. There must be a way to clearly resolve questions about the security and integrity of the system, process or reported results.

All of this requires strong political will for meaningful action. It also means we'll need to ensure the necessary money and expertise are available to make it happen in communities all across the country – admittedly not an easy task during a period of widespread budget constraints.

These concerns align with the basic principles of cybersecurity that apply to any organization. Information resources and their data must remain available and accessible to authorized users, confidential from unauthorized users, and protected from intentional and accidental tampering or modification. In meeting these challenges, organizations must find the resources to implement those safeguards in a proactive, effective, and ongoing fashion.

But there is a crucial difference that makes these particular cybersecurity efforts especially important: Election systems are truly critical foundations for our nation's underlying social and political infrastructure.

Rhetoric Attacked Legitimacy

Although this election does not appear to be "hacked" in the manner that many predicted, I do believe that it was successfully and directly attacked, repeatedly. These attacks did not come in the form of hackers altering vote counts. Rather, the attacks on this election's integrity came from assorted and perhaps nontraditional threats, both foreign and domestic.

Over the past year, Republican Donald Trump repeatedly made vague claims of a "rigged" system, possibly related to unsubstantiated allegations of widespread voter fraud or Russian influence. In addition, politically sensitive information was regularly revealed by groups and organizations believing themselves to be above the rules of law and common sense. And, the media itself became the recurring target of scorn as enablers of the alleged election "rigging."

These claims targeted the public's behavioral and cognitive systems. Consequently, many Americans believe that the voting "system" in America cannot be trusted – even though there is no such thing. Rather, the country's elections operate on a patchwork of local and state rules, procedures and technologies.

To wit: Some states use fully electronic voting while others retain the traditional paper ballot. Polls open and close at different times across the country. Some states may offer a window for early voting while others do not. There is no unified national election "system" that could be attacked or disrupted in a single effort.

Unfortunately, refuting claims of vote-rigging or offering contrary views – even when based on documented evidence – was dismissed by believers as further proof of a "rigged" system.

Oddly, Trump made these "rigging" claims despite the fact that he was the nominee of a party whose own members oversee voting matters in many states. That means his allegations suggested his own party's officials and election procedures were conspiring against him.

All this made it more difficult to discuss legitimate voting security concerns objectively, rationally or meaningfully. When everyone believes their own set of "facts," it is hard to address collective problems.

For these reasons, I believe election 2016 demonstrated the fragility of the American electoral process. It is susceptible to various types of attacks, overt and subtle, technical and nontechnical.

Protecting the Voting System

Efforts to protect the American voting system can learn from the practice of cybersecurity. Cybersecurity professionals work to prevent attacks, and to respond to those that happen, in several ways. They identify threats and vulnerabilities in their systems and networks. They create and execute procedures to operate those systems. And they otherwise work to provide a secure cyberspace for their organizations.

They also share threat information and best practices across companies and government agencies. This is because they recognize that cybersecurity is a shared responsibility and collective efforts are more helpful than working alone.

The electoral equivalent of this problem involves much more than identifying and reducing the technical vulnerabilities with electronic voting machines from their assembly all the way to when they're used on Election Day. We must also ensure the integrity of all election data and systems, from the time a citizen submits their personal information when registering to vote, through casting their ballot, and on into counting the vote, tabulating it, and having it formally recorded by state election officials.

Elections, like cybersecurity, are a shared effort involving many different people and organizations from industry and all levels of government. To carry the metaphor further, let's also take steps to ensure that the proverbial "window of vulnerability" is as small as possible. In the electoral process, reducing the potential time for an attacker to cause mischief is a valuable thing to consider. For example, is there really a need to have a multi-year presidential campaign that can be swayed regularly by any number of hacks in the cyber or cognitive domains?

Errors Still Happen

As of this evening, the process of voting appears to have encountered minimal, if any, cybersecurity-related problems. However, we may not learn about them immediately – unless attackers claim responsibility or government agencies make a public statement. Again, trust in the system, and trust in the people, processes and technologies, is crucial.

Yes, there will be human or procedural errors made in vote-casting and vote-counting. They, like any human process or organizational system, are not totally foolproof or errorproof. We must accept that fact. Will there be voter fraud somewhere? Perhaps. But in widespread numbers? Doubtful. And will votes be changed by overseas hackers? Probably not.

Certainly, there will be periodic and likely very minor errors, glitches, and hiccups in the overall election process – there almost always are. The media will report on them, social media will amplify them, and certain candidates or their supporters might use those reports as evidence of a larger conspiracy and evidence of a system "rigged" against them.

But even if tonight's vote count isn't hacked, the damage is done. We must acknowledge that the integrity of America's election system has been attacked successfully. Accordingly, once people have recovered from election 2016, we must implement a series of bipartisan, nationwide, rational and objective discussions about our election processes and technologies so that citizen trust in this most cherished national infrastructure – and feature of American democracy – can be restored.

CHAPTER 2

Did Russia's Interference Influence the 2016 US Election?

The Russian Involvement in the 2016 Election Is Complicated

Nilagia McCoy

Nilagia McCoy is the Communications Director at the Shorenstein Center on Media, Politics, and Public Policy.

Garrett Graff, journalist, author, and director of the Aspen Institute's cybersecurity and technology program, discussed Robert Mueller's investigations, election cybersecurity, and threats to U.S. democracy during a visit to the Shorenstein Center. Below are some highlights of his conversation with Shorenstein Center Director Nicco Mele. Graff, who has written about Mueller extensively, also discussed Mueller's background, career, and his leadership at the FBI.

Mysteries Remain Amid Media Coverage

"The thing that is most interesting to me about watching Bob Mueller do this investigation is how little we actually know about what Mueller is doing. This is the most carefully covered investigation in American history. On any given day, there are approximately 3,000 journalists in Washington desperately trying to find any tiny scrap of new information…In the midst of this political microscope, Bob Mueller arrested George Papadopoulos, got him to cooperate, and had him plead guilty without anyone in Washington realizing he was even a player in the investigation at that point."

"We know that there are at least two very significant pieces of evidence that Bob Mueller knows—we don't have any idea what they are—which is the information that George Papadopoulos traded for his plea deal, and the information that Michael Flynn traded for his plea deal. Under normal Justice Department procedure, you don't get much benefit from cooperating down, providing information on people lower in a conspiracy than you are. If you are the national security advisor at the White House, there are probably only about five people in the world that you could provide information to the Justice Department on that they would consider cooperating up. It's a testament to Mueller, as well as the team that he has assembled…I don't know of a single journalist that I've talked to who can point to a leak that seems like it's attributable to Bob Mueller's team, which is remarkable."

Understanding the Investigations

"We talk about the Mueller probe as if it's a single entity, but it's at least five different separate criminal probes. That's something I think we have lost track of."

"You have a distinct investigation and set of charges around past business deals and money laundering. This is the part of the investigation that has given rise to the charges against Paul Manafort and Rick Gates, for activity largely unrelated to the Trump campaign itself, but is sort of past business dealings with Russian and Ukrainian entities."

"Second, what we call the hacking of the election, is in fact two very distinct sets of Russian intelligence operations carried out by distinct Russian entities…this is the Facebook, Twitter bots and trolls, the fake news push, the data analytics work, voter targeting that was going on."

"Third is a separate part of the hacking of the election which is the active cyber intrusions, which were operations carried out by the Russian FSB and GRU, the hacking teams that we call Fancy Bear and Cozy Bear, that were active attempts to penetrate and weaponize information stolen from the DNC, the DCCC, Republican sites, also John Podesta's email, and state level voting infrastructure."

"Fourth is the suspicious Russian campaign contacts, and this is the weird milieu of Russian nationals and Russian officials, that involved everyone from random entertainment lawyers to the head of the VEB Russian bank…the head of that bank, Sergey Gorkov, is the person Jared Kushner meets with privately at Trump Tower after the election. Then obviously you have the contact with Russian Ambassador Sergey Kislyak, which is what forces Jeff Sessions to recuse himself from this investigation and is the center of Mike Flynn's plea deal."

"And then fifth, totally separate, is the big kahuna investigation, which is obstruction of justice…this is the question of whether Donald Trump or other aides at the White House either obstructed justice by pressuring James Comey to look past the Michael Flynn investigation, and then when Comey did not, fired him."

What's Next?

"I really hesitate to make predictions about where this investigation is going to go for a variety of obvious reasons…almost every stage of this has turned out to be weirder than we could have imagined. But I don't know that I have seen evidence that yet leads me to believe that on the Trump side, there was an active, engaged conspiracy. I think what you saw were a large number of opportunistic individuals working to advance their own agendas and their own power and business interests, in the midst of a uniquely chaotic and poorly organized campaign structure. Which is not to say that there was not on the Russian side an active conspiracy to influence the Trump campaign."

On Conservative Backlash Against Mueller

"I think you'd be hard pressed to find a more traditionally conservative institution in the United States than the FBI…When Bob Mueller was the leader of it he wore a white shirt every single day as FBI director because that's what J. Edgar Hoover wore every day as FBI director. That is not exactly the breeding ground for a George Soros-led Democratic secret society."

Hacking and the 2018 Midterms

"We are nowhere close to where we need to be in securing our election infrastructure. The good news/bad news is our election infrastructure is so confusing and antiquated, at scale it's going to be incredibly hard for a foreign entity to effect. The bad news is, in 2016, we just worried about Russia. Every other foreign adversary that the U.S. faces, from nation states to transnational groups, is looking at the midterm elections saying, 'oh, I have some new ideas.'"

"This is ultimately why I think the Republican Party's head in the sand with election interference is so troubling and so strange. There's no guarantee Russia's coming back on your side in the 2018 midterm elections. Vladimir Putin has a very specific set of goals…he is trying to tear down Western democracy and wants to destabilize it."

"There are all sorts of different problems that could happen on Election Day, none of which would fundamentally affect the integrity of the voting process. You don't need to actually get into a voting database. You could shut down every American looking up where to vote. You could do that district by district. You could shut down access to the Associated Press website the night of the election and make it three days before America realizes who won Congress. We have numerous ways we are uniquely vulnerable in our election infrastructure right now, and we're not doing anything about any of the different problems that we have."

Eroding Institutions

"I think it's incredibly dangerous, what we are seeing right now… Bob Mueller is an institutionalist, and democracy relies on the strength of its institutions. This is the thing that we have as a country. We don't have a monarchy, very specifically, we don't have a hereditary change of power. What we have are institutions that bind us together, generation by generation."

"If I can bring in my other book [*Raven Rock: The Story of the U.S. Government's Secret Plan to Save Itself—While the Rest of Us*

Die] about the history of the government's doomsday plans—one of the things that stood out for me about the U.S. government's plans for nuclear war, is that the government made a very conscious decision that it wasn't going to be enough to save the government. We needed to save the historical totems that have bound us together by generations. At the National Archives, they had a plan for saving the Declaration of Independence, and that they would save it before they saved the Constitution. At the Library of Congress, they had a plan to save the Gettysburg Address before they saved George Washington's Military Commission. Through the Cold War, in Philadelphia, there was a specially-trained team of park rangers whose job it was to evacuate the Liberty Bell in the event of a surprise Soviet attack. These are the things that make us Americans, and make us America, and it's not us, and it's not any single generation, and it's not any single president or any single Congress."

"What we are witnessing right now is the public destruction and denigration of institutions that we will need in a crisis, and when that crisis arises, which it will, we are going to be sad about what we have allowed the congressional Republicans and the Trump administration to do to critical American institutions."

Russia's Misinformation Warfare Influenced American Minds

Molly McKew

Molly McKew is a writer and expert in information warfare specializing in US-Russia relations.

For some time, there has been a conflation of issues—the hacking and leaking of illegally obtained information versus propaganda and disinformation; cyber-security issues and the hacking of elections systems versus information operations and information warfare; paid advertising versus coercive messaging or psychological operations—when discussing "Russian meddling" in the 2016 US elections. The refrain has become: "There is no evidence that Russian efforts changed any votes."

But the bombshell 37-page indictment issued Friday by Robert Mueller against Russia's Internet Research Agency and its leadership and affiliates provides considerable detail on the Russian information warfare targeting the American public during the elections. And this information makes it increasingly difficult to say that the Kremlin's effort to impact the American mind did not succeed.

The indictment pulls the curtain back on four big questions that have swirled around the Russian influence operation, which, it turns out, began in 2014: What was the scope of the Russian effort? What kind of content did it rely on? Who or what was it targeting, and what did it aim to achieve? And finally, what impact did it have?

Most of the discussion of this to date has focused on ideas of political advertising and the reach of a handful of ads—and this discussion has completely missed the point.

So let's take these questions one at a time.

"Did Russia Affect the 2016 Election? It's Now Undeniable," by Molly McKew, Condé Nast, February 16, 2018. Reprinted by permission.

What Was the Scope of the Russian Effort?

The Mueller indictment permanently demolishes the idea that the scale of the Russian campaign was not significant enough to have any impact on the American public. We are no longer talking about approximately $100,000 (paid in rubles, no less) of advertising grudgingly disclosed by Facebook, but tens of millions of dollars spent over several years to build a broad, sophisticated system that can influence American opinion.

The Russian efforts described in the indictment focused on establishing deep, authenticated, long-term identities for individuals and groups within specific communities. This was underlaid by the establishment of servers and VPNs based in the US to mask the location of the individuals involved. US-based email accounts linked to fake or stolen US identity documents (driver licenses, social security numbers, and more) were used to back the online identities. These identities were also used to launder payments through PayPal and cryptocurrency accounts. All of this deception was designed to make it appear that these activities were being carried out by Americans.

Additionally, the indictment mentions that the IRA had a department whose job was gaming algorithms. This is important because information warfare—the term used in the indictment itself—is not about "fake news" and "bots." It is about creating an information environment and a narrative—specific storytelling vehicles used to achieve goals of subversion and activation, amplified and promoted through a variety of means.

What Kind of Content Did It Rely on?

As the indictment lays out in thorough detail, the content pumped out by the Russians was not paid or promoted ads; it was so-called native content—including video, visual, memetic, and text elements designed to push narrative themes, conspiracies, and character attacks. All of it was designed to look like it was coming from authentic American voices and interest groups. And the IRA wasn't just guessing about what worked. They used data-driven targeting and analysis to assess how the content was received, and they used that information to refine their messages and make them more effective.

Who or What Was the Operation Targeting, and What Did It Aim to Achieve?

The indictment mentions that the Russian accounts were meant to embed with and emulate "radical" groups. The content was not designed to persuade people to change their views, but to harden those views. Confirmation bias is powerful and commonly employed in these kinds of psychological operations (a related Soviet concept is "reflexive control"—applying pressure in ways to elicit a specific, known response). The intention of these campaigns was to activate—or suppress—target groups. Not to change their views, but to change their behavior.

What Impact Did It Have?

We're only at the beginning of having an answer to this question because we've only just begun to ask some of the right questions. But Mueller's indictment shows that Russian accounts and agents accomplished more than just stoking divisions and tensions with sloppy propaganda memes. The messaging was more sophisticated, and some Americans took action. For example, the indictment recounts a number of instances where events and demonstrations were organized by Russians posing as Americans on social media. These accounts aimed to get people to do specific things. And it turns out—some people did.

Changing or activating behavior in this way is difficult; it's easier to create awareness of a narrative. Consistent exposure over a period of time has a complex impact on a person's cognitive environment. If groups were activated, then certainly the narrative being pushed by the IRA penetrated people's minds. And sure enough, the themes identified in the indictment were topics frequently raised during the election, and they were frequently echoed and promoted across social media and by conservative outlets. A key goal of these campaigns was "mainstreaming" an idea—moving it from the fringe to the mainstream and thus making it appear to be a more widely held than it actually is.

This points to another impact that can be extracted from the indictment: It is now much more difficult to separate what is "Russian" or "American" information architecture in the US information environment. This will make it far harder to assess where stories and narratives are coming from, whether they are real or propaganda, whether they represent the views of our neighbors or not.

This corrosive effect is real and significant. Which part of the fear of "sharia law in America" came from Russian accounts versus readers of InfoWars? How much did the Russian campaigns targeting black voters impact the low turnout, versus the character attacks run against Clinton by the Trump campaign itself? For now, all we can know is that there is shared narrative, and shared responsibility. But if, as the indictment says, Russian information warriors were instructed to support "Sanders and Trump," and those two campaigns appeared to have the most aggressive and effective online outreach, what piece of that is us, and what is them?

Persuasion and influence via social media cannot be estimated in linear terms; it requires looking at network effects. It is about the impact of a complex media environment with many layers, inputs, voices, amplifiers, and personalities. All of these elements change over time and interact with each other.

So anyone trying to tell you there was little impact on political views from the tools the Russians used doesn't know. Because none of us knows. No one has looked. Social media companies don't want us to know, and they obfuscate and drag their feet rather than disclosing information. The analytical tools to quantify the impact don't readily exist. But we know what we see, and what we heard—and the narratives pushed by the Russian information operation made it to all of our ears and eyes.

The groups and narratives identified in the indictment were integral parts of the frenzied election circus that built momentum, shaped perceptions, and activated a core base of support for now-President Trump—just as they helped disgust and dismay other groups, making them less likely to vote (or to vote for marginal candidates in protest).

In the indictment, Trump campaign officials are referred to as "unwitting" participants in Russian information warfare. This gives the White House an out—and a chance to finally act against what the Kremlin did. But the evidence presented in the indictment makes it increasingly hard to say Russian efforts to influence the American mind were a failure.

Russia's Interference Spotlights Weaknesses in US Election Process

Donna Brazile

Donna Brazile is an American political strategist, campaign manager, political analyst, and author.

> *"There should be no doubt that Russia perceives its past efforts as successful and views the 2018 U.S. midterm elections as a potential target for Russian influence operations."*
>
> —Dan Coats, Director of National Intelligence,
> February 13, 2018.

The 2016 presidential election was unlike any other. The contest had the look of a circus, with each news cycle driven by outrageous claims and scandalous events rather than an examination of the issues facing the nation. As a result, some voters didn't know who to believe or trust and stayed home on Election Day. The result was an election where the candidate who won the highest office in the land did not win the popular vote.

Since then we have come to know how much our fears and yearnings were manipulated by agents for the Russian government, and how few protections we have in place to prevent them from distorting our electoral process in the coming 2018 midterm elections and the 2020 presidential contest. The hacking of our electoral system poses a significant threat to our democracy by undermining faith in our public institutions such as the mainstream media, political parties, and statewide election systems and databases.

There was a time when, if a foreign power interfered in an American election, both major political parties would spring into action to protect the integrity of our election. That is not happening, and a 2017 Shorenstein Center survey of campaign managers and campaign staff members revealed how unprepared our political candidates are for the digital threats they face at election time. The results show that while those surveyed are aware of the cyber threats, many of them do not take them seriously.

The survey of nearly forty Republican and Democratic campaign operatives, administered through November and December 2017, revealed that American political campaign staff — primarily working at the state and congressional levels — are not only unprepared for possible cyber attacks, but remain generally unconcerned about the threat. The survey sample was relatively small, but nevertheless the survey provides a first look at how campaign managers and staff are responding to the threat.

The overwhelming majority of those surveyed do not want to devote campaign resources to cybersecurity or to hire personnel to address cybersecurity issues. Even though campaign managers recognize there is a high probability that campaign and personal emails are at risk of being hacked, they are more concerned about fundraising and press coverage than they are about cybersecurity. Less than half of those surveyed said they had taken steps to make their data secure and most were unsure if they wanted to spend any money on this protection.

Campaign officials should understand that their key assets in political campaigns, data and technologies, are at risk. Campaign staff, volunteers, and candidates should receive cyber education training. Our democracy is at risk. Cyber threats are constantly evolving, especially through the use of social media platforms. These "active measures," if not countered through training and a public education campaign, will erode confidence in the U.S. political system, destabilize campaigns, discredit candidates, and weaken both campaigns and election systems through deception, intraparty discord, and the spread of false information.

Background: The 2016 Election and Its Aftermath

On January 16, 2017, U.S. intelligence agencies concluded that "Russian President Vladimir Putin ordered an influence campaign in 2016 aimed at the U.S Presidential election." The goal, said the agencies, was to "undermine faith in the U.S. democratic process, denigrate Secretary Clinton, and harm her electability and potential presidency."

Nearly a year later, on February 16, 2018, Special Counsel Robert Mueller, who has been investigating Russian interference in the 2016 election, filed an indictment against 13 Russian nationals and 3 Russian organizations, which sought a specific outcome to the 2016 presidential election. The 37-page indictment reads like a spy novel with Russians posing as Americans to scout out our politics, setting up fake identities and shell companies to pay for demonstrations and rallies, and creating websites and bots that promoted then-candidates Donald Trump, Bernie Sanders, and Jill Stein.

The Democratic National Committee (DNC), along with the presidential campaign of Hillary Clinton (HFA), the Democratic Congressional Campaign Committee (DCCC), and private individuals — plus other entities with the responsibility for keeping statewide databases, voter registration, and electronic poll books — became the targets of a sophisticated cyber hacking operation that sought to sow discord, weaponize hacked emails, create chaos at the ballot box, and undermine faith in the integrity of the election and its outcome.

As Americans prepare for the 2018 midterm election, where there are 435 seats in the U.S. House of Representatives, 34 Senate seats, and 36 gubernatorial seats up for grabs, neither President Donald Trump nor Congress has fully acknowledged the assault on American democracy nor taken credible steps to protect, educate, and prepare American voters on Russian threats to future elections.

President Trump continues to label each investigation into the Russian meddling as a "witch hunt" or "a total hoax" created by his opponents. He refuses to accept the findings of the intelligence agencies. Trump appears unbothered by the threat posed by Russia's attack on our democracy, even as we learn more about its efforts to divide our country and create chaos. In response to the Mueller indictment, Trump issued not a call to action, but a vindication of himself. He tweeted, "Russia started their anti-US campaign in 2014, long before I announced that I would run for President. The results of the election were not impacted. The Trump campaign did nothing wrong — no collusion!"

Both houses of Congress have undertaken investigations into Russian interference in the 2016 presidential election. On April 27, 2018, the House Intelligence Committee concluded its yearlong investigation and issued a report that declared that the Trump campaign did not collude with Russia or aid in Russia's meddling in the presidential election. The Senate's investigation remains ongoing. To date, legislation to address Russia's intrusions remain in their formative, initial stages. However, a bill imposing new sanctions on Russia for its behavior in the Ukraine and its meddling in the 2016 election passed the House 419-3 on July 25, 2017. Democrats have introduced the Election Security Act (on February 14, 2018 in the U.S. House) to help states restore the integrity and privacy of our elections. The law provides grants to states to enable them to update and secure their election infrastructure, but so far it has little to no support from Republicans.

Meanwhile, several states are taking actions to upgrade their electronic voting systems, electronic poll books, and the like to protect against malicious hardware and software vulnerabilities. During the summer of 2017, the National Council of State Legislators (NCSL) convened a major conference to discuss steps to protect the electoral integrity of their systems. One of their recommendations is the creation of a Cybersecurity Task Force to ensure state lawmakers are acutely aware of the threat posed to future elections. NCSL is working closely with the Department of Homeland Security (DHS) to build cyber literacy among state officials and to train state election officials.

With evidence continuing to mount that Russia did indeed attempt to influence the 2016 election, coordination continues to lag at both the federal and state levels where election administration is managed.

The Challenge in Western Democracies

During his testimony to Congress in June 2017, former FBI Director James Comey warned, "it's not a Republican thing or a Democratic thing. It really is an American thing." Comey added, "They're going to come for whatever party they choose to try and work on behalf of, and they're not devoted to either, in my experience. They're just about their own advantage and they will be back."

The United States is not alone in being under attack. The tactics used by the Russians in the United States were perfected after earlier efforts to meddle in the elections of other Western democracies. Within the European Union (EU), Russia has been accused of directly and indirectly engaging in a surreptitious, continent-wide effort to undermine pro-European groups, particularly in the Ukraine and France. Russia's state-owned media have constantly lauded the efforts of far right, anti-EU political parties including those in Holland, France, Germany, and most recently in Austria. The Russian disinformation campaign continues to amplify stories harmful to political leaders and parties that are strongly in favor of the European Union, NATO, and other pro-Western groups.

The U.S. has seen "initial signs" of Russian "subversion and disinformation and propaganda" in the Mexican presidential campaign. In this context, then-National Security Adviser H.R. McMaster said: "...with Russia we are concerned, increasingly concerned, with these sophisticated campaigns of subversion and disinformation and propaganda, the use of cyber tools to do that." According to a clip of his speech obtained by José Díaz Briseño, *Reforma*'s U.S. correspondent, McMaster said: "As you've seen this is a really sophisticated effort to polarize democratic societies and pit communities within those societies against each other and create crises of confidence and to undermine the strength within Europe. You see this most recently with the Catalonia independence referendum in Spain, for example. You see actually initial signs of it in the Mexican presidential campaign already."

Former President George W. Bush has repeatedly spoken out on the dangers of Russian interference. According to a *USA Today* report, Bush stated, "It's problematic that a foreign nation is involved in our election system. Our democracy is only as good as people trust the results."

The 2018 U.S. Midterm Elections: Are We Ready?

In 2018, American voters will go back to the polls to elect 36 governors, 34 U.S. Senators and 435 members of the U.S. House of Representatives. The integrity of our electoral system remains vulnerable to attack. The stakes are high.

Jeh Johnson, former director of the Department of Homeland Security, stated that the U.S. was "on alert on Election Day and in the days leading up to it, along with the FBI." Johnson commented that "…33 states and 36 cities and counties came to the Department before the 2016 election to seek their cybersecurity assistance. In working with those states, DHS helped to address a number of vulnerabilities in election infrastructure." He added, "I'm concerned that we are almost as vulnerable perhaps now as we were six, nine months ago."

One way to prepare for the upcoming elections is to provide state and local election officials with resources to address threats to IT systems and voting technology. In 2017, the House Democrats launched an Election Security Task Force headed by Representatives Bennie Thompson (D-MS) and Robert Brady (D-PA). They issued a report that identified ten specific recommendations on what the federal government and states can and should be doing to secure our nation's elections.

The Secure Elections Act was introduced on December 21, 2017, in the U.S. Senate by a bipartisan group of lawmakers led by Senators James Lankford (R-OK), Amy Klobuchar (D-MN), Lindsey Graham (R-SC), Kamala Harris (D-CA), Susan Collins (R-ME) and Martin Heinrich (D-NM). The Secure Elections

Act would mandate DHS to share more information with state and local election officials about threats to their IT systems or voting machines. The bill would also set up an expert panel to draft voluntary risk management guidelines and best practices that state and local agencies can use. Finally, it would authorize a $386 million grant program to help states implement these guidelines and replace outdated electronic voting machines.

In addition, The Securing America's Voting Equipment (SAVE) Act was introduced on October 31, 2017, by Senators Susan Collins (R-ME) and Martin Heinrich (D-NM). In a press release accompanying introduction of the legislation, the Senators noted that "[i]ntelligence assessments that Russian actors targeted state election voting centers and state-level voter registration databases as part of Russia's larger hostile effort to interfere in last year's election demonstrate a vulnerability to future cyber-attacks and manipulations by foreign hackers in our democratic process. The SAVE Act would facilitate information sharing with states, provide guidelines for how best to secure election systems, and allow states to access funds to develop their own solutions to the threats posed to elections."

In January 2018, all Democratic members of the House Committee on Oversight and Government Reform sent a letter asking Chairman Trey Gowdy to issue a subpoena to finally compel the Department of Homeland Security (DHS) to produce documents it has been withholding from Congress for months related to Russian government-backed efforts to monitor, penetrate, or otherwise hack at least 21 state election systems in the 2016 election. DHS has failed to provide the requested information, but the agency has confirmed that Russia was behind the attacks.

Social Media Platforms: The Big Unknown

It's clear from recent revelations that Russian meddling on social media platforms like Google, Facebook, and Twitter was extensive during the 2016 election. Whether it swayed the election is a hard question to answer, but what we do know is that millions — and potentially tens of millions — of American voters were exposed to content pushed by Russia in an election that was decided by just tens of thousands of votes. And it hasn't stopped, meaning its effect on 2018 and 2020 could be just as pernicious.

Social media platforms have been slow to acknowledge the situation and, until recently, reluctant to do anything about it. In some cases, their policies and actions may have caused valuable information to be lost about the Russian attacks, which often aimed to divide America on race, guns, immigration, religion, and other issues.

As detailed in *Politico*, Twitter was one of the most effectively exploited weapons by the Russian government to undermine Hillary Clinton's campaign and to help Donald Trump in the 2016 race. Kremlin-backed operatives used targeted ad buys, fake users, and automated bots to spread disinformation and false stories. Even so, Twitter's privacy policies for consumers may have resulted in the loss of tweets and data that would be invaluable to investigators trying to see how the Russian operation was carried out. Twitter failed to crack down on suspicious activity, and then allowed the data about that activity to be lost.

Senator Mark Warner, the ranking Democrat on the Senate Intelligence Committee that is investigating Russian interference, said Twitter's response had been "inadequate." According to Senator Warner, Twitter did only the bare minimum of investigating when it came to looking into the activity of the Russians on their platform.

As reported in *The New York Times*, members of the Congressional Black Caucus are just as angry about Facebook's response. Caucus Chair Cedric L. Richmond (D-LA) stated that "[the Caucus] needed Facebook to understand that they [Facebook] play a role in the perception of African-Americans."

Russian-backed operatives made substantial ad buys on Facebook that were aimed at inflaming racial and political divisions at a time when members of the African-American community were trying to highlight problems of systemic racism in the nation's justice system. Meanwhile, the foreign actors were using targeted Facebook ads to make white voters hostile to African-Americans' message and to exploit racial tension and mistrust.

The Senate Intelligence Committee summoned attorneys for Twitter, Facebook, and Google for a public hearing on November 1, 2017, to discuss how Russia may have used their sites to influence the 2016 election. The issue became more pressing for legislators in March 2018 after it was revealed that the personal data of millions of Facebook users was improperly shared with the political data firm Cambridge Analytica, which, in turn, used that data to advance President Trump's campaign. Mark Zuckerberg, CEO and Chairman of Facebook, was called to testify before the Senate Committee on the Judiciary and the Senate Committee on Commerce, Science and Transportation.

Zuckerberg appeared before the joint Senate Committee on April 10, 2018, and testified that Facebook "didn't do enough" to prevent misuse of its platform during the 2016 election. Zuckerberg elaborated: "That goes for fake news, foreign interference in elections, and hate speech, as well as developers and data privacy. We didn't take a broad enough view of our responsibility, and that was a big mistake. It was my mistake, and I'm sorry. I started Facebook, I run it, and I'm responsible for what happens here."

Zuckerberg further testified that Facebook "should have spotted Russian interference earlier," and that it is taking steps to prevent future interference by hostile foreign actors. Zuckerberg's contrition and the fact that Facebook appears serious about making changes to its security and advertising policies are critical first steps to preventing misuse of the social media site in future U.S. elections.

Prior to Zuckerberg's hearing, Senators Warner (D-VA), McCain (R-AZ), and Klobuchar (D-MN) introduced the Honest Ads Act that aims to "prevent foreign interference in future elections and improve the transparency of online political advertisements." Days before his Senate hearing, Zuckberberg endorsed the Act and Twitter soon followed. This legislation is important for the preservation of our democracy because it will inhibit foreign powers from polluting the internet with fabricated stories and disinformation.

Faced with the president's denial and the sluggish response by the tech community, it's more vital than ever that Congress step into the void to raise the alarm and to apply pressure to social media companies through the current Russia investigations and possible legislative remedies.

Are Campaigns Equipped To Maintain Cyber Safety?

Over the past year, the world has become increasingly aware of the importance of cybersecurity for political systems and governments. From Russian infiltration of the 2016 presidential elections in the U.S., to emails from top political leaders leaked to the public, political operatives must be better prepared to protect the integrity of online data and information.

How Do Campaign Staffers View This Threat?

After the hacking of the 2016 election, it's not surprising that nearly all the campaign staff surveyed (92%) were familiar with news about cyber meddling in political campaigns and party offices during the 2016 election cycle. Nearly two-thirds are aware of the practice of fraudulent emails sent under the guise of a trusted colleague to gather confidential information from targeted individuals (known as spear phishing). Perhaps the most famous example of spear phishing was the hacking of Hillary Clinton campaign chairman John Podesta's emails.

The concern about hacking and interference is quite high among the campaign staffers surveyed. Indeed, 81 percent said that they are either "somewhat" or "very concerned" about stories reporting the hacking of campaigns and party offices. Fewer than 1 in 5 (18%) reported they are not concerned.

Nevertheless, these same campaign staffers are much less concerned about foreign actors meddling in their own campaigns. Two-thirds (65%) reported they are not "very concerned" or "not concerned at all" about foreign threats to campaign cybersecurity.

What Have Campaigns Done To Prepare For Cyber Attacks, And What Are They Willing To Do To Prevent Them?

When asked about concerns and obstacles on the campaign trail, the hacking of campaign files and emails ranked second to last, only above the risk of not receiving key endorsements. Campaign staffers are mostly concerned about losing the election or not raising enough money. Other areas of concern included an inability to hire enough qualified staffers, the candidate making a gaffe, and receiving bad press. High-level staffers generally ranked these issues as a much bigger concern to their campaigns than cyber interference.

These same campaign staffers are generally confident in the security of their campaign files and databases (voter files, donor records, etc.). Half of respondents reported it would be "somewhat" (37%) or "very" (14%) difficult for someone to hack their campaign files, and even more believed it would be "somewhat" (43%) or "very" (20%) difficult for someone to hack their campaign databases. However, the campaign operatives' perspectives shifted when asked about email; half of the campaign operatives studied think it would be "somewhat" (46%) or "very" (9%) easy for someone to hack their campaign emails.

When it comes to their preparedness compared to other campaigns, staffers generally feel they are about as well-equipped as most campaigns (64%), while only 19 percent think that their current campaign is better equipped than other campaigns. Eleven percent of those surveyed believe they are less equipped compared to other campaigns and 6 percent are unsure.

The lack of seriousness with which these staffers regard campaigns' cyber defense becomes clearer as campaigns report their willingness to spend money on added protections. Nearly half said their campaigns are willing to spend less than $5,000 on added protections against hacking, and 34 percent were not certain how much they would be willing to spend.

When asked whether their campaign has taken steps to prevent their network and emails from being hacked, nearly half (40%) shared they "have taken steps to protect their campaigns," while 31 percent say they have "not yet but plan on doing so in the future." Just 11 percent say they "do not plan" on taking these steps.

A majority of staffers surveyed have taken concrete steps toward more effective campaign security. The most common best practices include requiring passwords for staff, installing antivirus software on all campaign devices, setting up firewalls, requiring two-step verification, requiring password standards for consultants and volunteers, and not allowing campaign staff, volunteers, or consultants to use thumb drives — especially important since nearly half of campaign staffers (46%) believe that "at least" some volunteers on their campaigns have access to data.

Despite this, staffers are still relatively ill-prepared. The campaign operatives surveyed have not generally set up firewalls, required passwords for staff, or hired a designated staff person for information or data security. Just over two-thirds (69%) have neither hired a Chief Information Security Officer, nor an equivalent staffer. The same amount do not actively use tabletop exercises (a simulated emergency situation) to train their IT staff how to assess and respond to network vulnerabilities.

Conclusion

While Congress completes its investigations into the 2016 presidential election, it is vital that we prepare state election officials, candidates, and their campaigns to protect themselves from cyber threats.

The White House recently announced that President Trump convened a meeting with top intelligence and legal officials to discuss the administration's plans to secure state and local election systems and to protect them from malign foreign influence. The administration's acknowledgment that election security is directly related to our national security is a critical first step in securing our elections and, more importantly, it may raise cybersecurity awareness among state and local campaigns.

The Shorenstein Center survey shows that while campaign staffs are well aware of the threat posed by cyber attacks, most are more concerned with other things, such as raising enough money or receiving bad press. They fail to recognize, as the 2016 election revealed, that a cyber attack that exposes campaign data can depress fundraising, inhibit endorsements, and create weeks of bad press.

Despite this, few campaigns have invested in cybersecurity efforts like hiring a chief information security officer or using tabletop exercises to train staff. The vital tools of modern campaigns — internet-enabled devices, software, and connectivity — need as much protection as the voting box, yet staffs and party leaders show that digital protection is not a high priority.

The threat of cyber attacks cannot be eliminated. Nevertheless, campaigns must practice vigilance and view IT and cybersecurity across the campaign organization as a necessity. Campaigns will need to adopt the necessary tools to protect against these threats and expand their budgets and staff. If not, campaigns and elections will continue to be highly vulnerable to hacking and interference.

Russia's Ambassador Refutes Russian Interference Accusations

Tasnim News Agency

Tasnim News Agency is a leading news agency in Iran. It covers a wide variety of political, social, economic, and international subjects along with other topics in an effort to boost public knowledge and awareness both inside and outside the country.

C BS News had a conversation with the new Russian ambassador to the US about the investigation into Russian interference in the 2016 presidential election.

Ambassador Anatoloy Antonov told CBS News' Margaret Brennan the probe severely complicates his work. Many US officials even refuse to meet him.

"Mr. Trump made it clear many times so that he would like to improve Russian-American relations, but 'til now I couldn't say that our relations become better," Antonov said. "I see unpredictability every morning. I don't know what to do because I am waiting other negative steps from administration."

"How do you possibly get past the mistrust around the 2016 election?" Brennan asked.

"It's very difficult to try to find a black cat in dark room where it is no any cat at all," Antonov said.

"You're saying there's no story there?" Brennan asked.

"There is no any proof regarding Russian interference into your election," he said.

Hours before CBS News' interview, Trump's former national security adviser Michael Flynn pleaded guilty to lying to the FBI about his contacts with Antonov's predecessor, Sergey Kislyak.

"Russia's Ambassador Says There Is No Proof of Moscow Interference in US Election," Tasmin News Agency, December 5, 2017. https://www.tasnimnews.com/en/news/2017/12/05/1592847/russia-s-ambassador-says-there-is-no-proof-of-moscow-interference-in-us-election. Licensed under CC BY 4.0 International.

"Frankly, I don't understand why any officials has no any right to speak to Russian ambassador," he said.

"What do you make of that? I mean these are serious charges involving your previous ambassador — that complicates things," Brennan said.

"Yes. He is smart, talented diplomat," Antonov said. "And I very much surprised that some mass media decided to blame him as a spy. It's stupid. It's nonsense."

"Well, this is the FBI," Brennan said.

"No, come on you'll say that," Antonov said.

Antonov dismissed it as a political disagreement within the US.

"It seems to me that this atmosphere is poisoned but by some officials, excuse me, maybe some journalists, who want to find a new enemy for the United States," Antonov said. "What we want, we want to be together, fighting terrorism to protect non-proliferation and maybe to start negotiations about— negotiations regarding nuclear disarmament."

Antonov, who has brokered arms control deals with the US before, also told CBS News he wants to collaborate on cyber security. So far, that offer has not been taken up by the US.

Russia Ignores the Threat of Sanctions for Election Interference

Charles Maynes

Charles Maynes is a contributing producer with the Foundation for Independent Radio Broadcasting (FNR), an NGO that works for the development of quality public programming in Russia.

Russian officials, including President Vladimir Putin, poured scorn over the United States' publication of the so-called "oligarchs list" — a US Treasury-issued registry of 210 Russians identified as close to Putin under a new sanctions law that resulted from allegations of Kremlin interference in the 2016 US presidential elections.

Speaking in Moscow, Putin said that by including nearly all key members of his government and Russian industry on the list the US had, in effect, carried out "a hostile step" against "all 146 million Russians." His only regret, the Russian leader added, was that he wasn't among them on the list.

Yet Putin indicated that Russia would not respond — for now.

"We're not prepared to crawl into the wolf's trap and make the situation worse," said Putin. "We want and will patiently build relations as much as the American side is willing."

The list — part of the wider Countering America's Adversaries Through Sanctions Act (CAATSA) ordered by Congress and signed into law by President Donald Trump last August — requires the White House to provide a detailed report on the dealings of key Kremlin insiders.

However, the Trump administration — which has bristled at suggestions it benefited from Russian interference in the US elections — held off on complying with the law until the last minute.

"Russia reacts to the 'oligarch list'," by Charles Maynes, Public Radio International, January 30, 2018. Reprinted by permission.

On Tuesday afternoon, US Treasury Secretary Steven Mnuchin told lawmakers that the Trump administration intends to levy new sanctions based on the list published late Monday.

Meanwhile, in Moscow, Russia's elite insisted any intended scare tactic wasn't working.

Vyacheslav Volodin, speaker of the Russian Duma, said the list was the latest in a failed US sanctions policy aimed at weakening an increasingly powerful Russia.

"The sanctions haven't led to a change in our country's political course, or weakened our sovereignty, or led to an internal split," said Volodin, in a statement posted to the Duma's official website. "New sanctions against Russia will lead to even greater consolidation of society," he added.

Konstantin Kosachev, the head of Russia's Federation Council Foreign Affairs Committee, mocked what he saw as amateur detective work by US intelligence agencies. Writing on Facebook, Kosachev said he had the "the firm impression that US secret services, desperate to find the provable compromising evidence they promised on Russian politicians, just copied the Kremlin phonebook."

Indeed, the US Treasury list of Russian oligarchs appeared to steal from a Forbes Russia ranking of the country's wealthiest 96 men; its registry of government figures, other journalists noted, was a near copy of the Kremlin's own English-language "key officials" webpage.

Even some Kremlin critics admitted that the sanctions were unlikely to unnerve Russia's powerful — at least not yet.

"It's a threat, not a punch," wrote Gudkov on his Facebook page. "For now that list only means a morning heart attack for the most sensitive of souls."

Election Interference Cuts Both Ways

In advance of the list's publication, the Kremlin had indicated Russia viewed the registry — and any additional sanctions — as an attempt by the US to influence Russia's presidential elections in March, when President Putin is all but guaranteed to win re-election to a 4th term in office.

Indeed, Putin was asked about the issue during a campaign meeting with supporters, one of whom asked what he would have to do to join the list — to audience laughter.

Putin responded by suggesting that Russians' goal should be to develop their economy to the point where "there's no point to formulating any lists ... to hold us back."

Yet Russia's opposition leader Alexey Navalny — who has been barred from competing in the presidential elections — was among those cheering the "Putin list" as long overdue.

Navalny noted that his Anti-Corruption Foundation team had carried out its own investigations — and produced reports that highlighted Kremlin corruption by several figures featured in the US Treasury list.

"Well, what I can say?" Navalny wrote on Twitter. "We're glad that they've been officially recognized as thieves and swindlers on the international level."

Meanwhile, online debate seemed to split over the blanket nature of the Treasury list and whether it had gone too far, or not far enough.

Why, some asked, hadn't the Kremlin central bankers been included? Where were Russia's senior court judges? The head of the Election Commission?

What, others wondered, was Russia's human rights ombudsman doing on the list? Or a businessman who, while wealthy, had no clear ties to the Kremlin?

And if Russia's top diplomat — Foreign Minister Sergey Lavrov — was on the list, others asked who would be left to negotiate with Washington if and when Russia were ever to repair relations.

Konstantin von Eggert, a foreign affairs analyst and host on the independent station TV Rain, noted that the list had suddenly rendered the role of competing interest groups inside and outside the Kremlin irrelevant.

Fairly or not, the US had included nearly Russia's entire political and economic elite in a web of Russia sanctions that touch on issues such as election interference, human rights abuses and the Kremlin's actions in Ukraine.

"Everyone," argued von Eggert, "is now in the same boat."

CHAPTER 3

Are Social Media and Fake News Responsible for 2016 Election Interference?

Social Media Has Changed the Way We Discuss Politics

Sam Sanders

Sam Sanders is a reporter and host of It's Been a Minute with Sam Sanders at NPR. In the show, Sanders engages with journalists, actors, musicians, and listeners to gain the kind of understanding about news and popular culture that can only be reached through conversation.

I've noticed two distinct ways social media have changed the way we talk to each other about politics. Clearly, they have changed a lot, maybe *everything*, but two fairly new phenomena stand out.

One happens on Facebook all the time. Just about all of your friends are posting about the election, nonstop. And there are a few who brag about deleting friends, or who urge friends to unfriend them over their political leanings: "Just unfriend me now." Or something like "If you can't support candidate X/Y, we don't need to be friends anymore." Or "Congrats, if you're reading this, you survived my friend purge!" Etc. You know how it goes. This public declaration, if not celebration, of the end of *friendships* because of politics.

And then on Twitter, there's the public shaming of those who dare disagree with or insult you. (I am guilty of this.) Someone tweets at you with something incendiary, bashing the article you just shared or the point you just made, mocking something you said about politics, calling you stupid. You quote the tweet, maybe sarcastically, to prove it doesn't affect you. But it does! You tweeted it back, to all of your followers. It's an odd cycle. A rebuttal of nasty political exchanges by highlighting nasty political exchanges.\ This is our present political social life: We don't just create political strife for ourselves; we seem to revel in it.

When we look back on the role that sites like Twitter, Facebook (and Instagram and Snapchat and all the others) have played in our national political discourse this election season, it would be easy to spend most of our time examining Donald Trump's effect on these media, particularly Twitter. It's been well-documented; Trump may very well have the most combative online presence of any candidate for president in modern history.

But underneath that glaring and obvious conclusion, there's a deeper story about how the very DNA of social media platforms and the way people use them has trickled up through our political discourse and affected all of us, almost *forcing* us to wallow in the divisive waters of our online conversation. And it all may have helped make Election 2016 one of the most unbearable ever.

A Problem with Format

Fully understanding just how social media have changed our national political conversation means understanding what these platforms were initially intended to do, and how we use them now.

At its core, Twitter is a messaging service allowing users (who can remain anonymous) to tweet out information, or opinions, or whatever, in 140-character bursts. For many critics, that DNA makes Twitter antithetical to sophisticated, thoughtful political conversation.

"Both the technology itself, and the way we choose to use the technology, makes it so that what ought to be a conversation is just a set of Post-it notes that are scattered," Kerric Harvey, author of the *Encyclopedia of Social Media and Politics,* said of Twitter. "Not even on the refrigerator door, but on the ground."

She argues that what we do on Twitter around politics isn't a conversation at all; it's a loud mess.

Bridget Coyne, a senior manager at Twitter, points to several features the company has added to those 140-character tweets: polls, photos, video, Moments and more. She also told NPR that the 140-character limit reflects the app's start as a mobile-first platform, and that it's different now. "We've evolved into a website and many other platforms from that." And she, like every other spokesman for any major social media platform, argues that sites like Twitter have *democratized* the political conversation, helping give everyone a voice, and that's a good thing.

But even accepting that point, and respecting every new addition to Twitter's list of tools, we find a way to keep arguing. Even the candidates do it.

One particular exchange between Hillary Clinton and Jeb Bush (remember him?) illustrates this new political reality. On Aug. 10, 2015, Clinton's Twitter account posted a graphic with the words: "$1.2 trillion, the amount 40 million Americans owe in student debt."

Jeb Bush's campaign replied, tweaking Clinton's own graphic to read "100%, The increase in student debt under this Democratic White House."

Those two tweets seem reasonable enough. But there was more. In response to the Bush campaign's response, Team Clinton scratched out the words in Bush's redone graphic, added its own scribbled letters, and etched a large "F" on top, for the "grade given to Florida for college affordability under Jeb Bush's leadership." The campaign tweeted the image with the caption "Fixed it for you."

And *then,* the Bush account replied once more, turning Clinton's "H" logo, with its right-pointing arrow, by 90 degrees, sending the arrow point skyward, with the word "taxes" printed behind over and over. That caption was "fixed your logo for you."

It was an exchange nearing petty; these two candidates were trolling each other. But for the most part it seemed totally normal in a campaign season like this one, and in the digital age in which we live. Establishment political figures like Bush and Clinton (or at least their young staffers) had co-opted the language of social media and mastered the formats, with all the snark and back and forth that come along with it, and with an extra incentive to adopt some of the meanness Trump has exhibited online.

There may be even more problems for Twitter than what real live people are doing on the app. A recent study conducted by a research team at Oxford University found that during the period of time between the first presidential debate and the second, one-third of pro-Trump tweets and nearly one-fifth of pro-Clinton tweets came from automated accounts. Douglas Guilbeault, one of the researchers in the study, told NPR that hurts political discourse. "They reinforce the sense of polarization in the atmosphere," he said. "Because bots don't tend to be mild-mannered, judicial critics. They are programmed to align themselves with an agenda that is unambiguously representative of a particular party. ... It's all 'Crooked Hillary' and 'Trump is a puppet.' "

So, if Twitter is a bunch of Post-it notes thrown on the ground, we now have to consider which of those notes are even *real*.

The company would not offer its own estimate on the number of bots on its app, or any on-the-record rebuttal to the study's findings, besides the following statement: "Anyone claiming that spam accounts on Twitter are distorting the national, political conversation is misinformed."

Even if there are questions about the number of bots on Twitter, the tone of the conversation there increasingly can't be denied. A recent study from the Anti-Defamation League found "a total of 2.6 million tweets containing language frequently found in anti-Semitic speech were posted across Twitter between August 2015 and July 2016," with many aimed at political journalists. And a Bloomberg report found trolling on the service is keeping the company from finding a buyer.

Facebook and the "Echo Chamber"

Facebook fares no better in garnering scathing critique of its influence on the political conversation. At its core, it's a platform meant to connect users with people they already like, not to foster discussion with those you might disagree with.

Facebook's News Feed, which is how most users see content through the app and site, is more likely to prominently display content based on a user's previous interests, and it also conforms to his or her political ideology. A Wall Street Journal interactive from May of this year shows just how much your feed is affected by your political leanings.

The company also faced rebuke from conservatives when it tried to share trending news stories on users' homepages; they said the shared articles reflected a liberal bias. And after trying unsuccessfully to begin filtering out fake news stories from users' feeds, Facebook has been increasingly accused of becoming a hotbed of fake political news. The most recent allegation comes from a BuzzFeed report, which found that a good amount of fake — and trending — Donald Trump news is coming from business-savvy millennials. In Macedonia.

In response to these critiques, Facebook pointed NPR to a September post from the company's CEO, Mark Zuckerberg, in which he said, "Whatever TV station you might watch or whatever newspaper you might read, on Facebook you're hearing from a broader set of people than you would have otherwise."

In that same post, Zuckerberg also pointed out studies showing that increasingly, more young people are getting their news primarily from sites like Facebook, and that young people have also said it helps them see a "larger and more diverse set of opinions." And Zuckerberg said the company is trying to do a better job of sifting out fake news.

Late last month, Facebook COO Sheryl Sandberg said Facebook had helped more than 2 million people register to vote.

It's Not Just the Social Networks

Social networks are built the way they're built, but how we've used them this year says just as much about our shortcomings as about any particular network's flaws.

Data tracking trending topics and themes on social networks over the course of the campaign show that for the most part, America was less concerned with policy than with everything else. Talkwalker, a social media analytics company, found that the top three political themes across social media platforms during the past year were Trump's comments about women, Clinton's ongoing email scandal, and Trump's refusal to release his tax returns.

"Social media may have played a role in creating a kind of scandal-driven, as opposed to issue-driven, campaign," said Todd Grossman, CEO of Talkwalker Americas, "where topics such as Trump's attitude towards women, Trump's tax returns and Clinton's emails have tended to dominate discussion as opposed to actual policy issues."

And Brandwatch, another company that tracks social media trends, found that on Twitter, from the time Trump and Clinton formally began their campaigns for president, aside from conversation around the three presidential debates, only two policy-driven conversations were in their top 10 most-tweeted days. Those were Trump calling for a complete ban on Muslims entering the United States, and Trump visiting Mexico and delivering a fiery immigration speech in Arizona in the span of 24 hours. Brandwatch found that none of Clinton's 10 biggest days on Twitter centered on policy, save for the debates. (And even in that debate conversation, topics like "nasty woman" and "bad hombres" outpaced others.)

Looking to the Future

So we end this campaign season with social media platforms seemingly hardwired for political argument, obfuscation and division. We are a public more concerned with scandal than policy, at least according to the social media data. And our candidates for higher office, led by Trump, seem more inclined to adopt the combative nature of social media than ever before.

It's too late to fix these problems for this election, but a look to the social networks of tomorrow might offer some hope.

Snapchat has emerged as the social network of the future. Data from Public Opinion Strategies find that more than 60 percent of U.S. smartphone owners ages 18 to 34 are using Snapchat and that on any given day, Snapchat reaches 41 percent of all 18- to 34-year-olds in the U.S. Any hope for the social media discourse of the future may be found with them.

Peter Hamby, head of news at Snapchat, says the platform is a "fundamentally different" experience than other social media platforms, in part because, he says, on Snapchat, privacy is key. "I think that people want to have a place where they can communicate with their friends and have fun, but also feel safe," Hamby said.

He also said he is working on figuring out what young people want in a social network and how to make it better. And, he said, social media users increasingly want to rely on their social networks to make sense of the flood of political opinions, reporting and vitriol they're being bombarded with. "One thing that me and my team have tried to do," Hamby told NPR, "is explain the election. ... Because a lot of stuff you see on the Web, and TV, is pretty noisy."

In asking whether social media ruined this election or not, I had to ask myself how my actions on social media have helped or hurt the country's political dialogue — what my contribution to all that noise has been. I'd have to say that even when I've tried to help, I'm not sure I've done enough.

Last month, I shared an article about something political on Twitter. Two women got into an argument in the replies to my tweet. I could tell that they didn't know each other, and that they were supporting different candidates for president. Every tweet they hurled back and forth at each other mentioned me, so I got notifications during every step of their online fight. At one point, they began to call each other names, with one young woman calling the other the "C" word.

I stepped in, told the two that they maybe should take a break from Twitter for a bit, do something else (or at least remove me from their mentions). Both responded. They apologized to each other and to me, and they both promised to log off for a bit. One mentioned trying to play a role in creating a nicer world after the election.

I left it at that, but should I have done more? Should I have urged the two to message each other privately, try to talk politics civilly, maybe think about ways to have enriching, productive conversations online (or better yet, in person)? Should I have asked myself if the words I used in sharing the original article helped lead to the argument? Should the three of us have made it a teachable moment?

Instead, they retreated from their battle positions for a few hours at best, never getting to know the stranger they insulted. And I moved on, and just kept tweeting.

But I had to, right? Making the social Web nicer always takes a back seat to just trying to keep up. There were more tweets to see, more stuff to read, more Internet Post-it notes to throw along our social media floor.

If social media ruined 2016, it's because of that: We haven't stopped long enough to try to sort it all out.

Social Media Filters and Algorithms Influence Voters

Alex Hern

Alex Hern is an insightful digital journalist, a talented writer, and a canny analyst for the Guardian. *He excels at both finding the best angle to engage readers on important topics and at digging into seemingly frivolous subjects to detail why they matter.*

One of the most powerful players in the British election is also one of the most opaque. With just over two weeks to go until voters go to the polls, there are two things every election expert agrees on: what happens on social media, and Facebook in particular, will have an enormous effect on how the country votes; and no one has any clue how to measure what's actually happening there.

"Many of us wish we could study Facebook," said Prof Philip Howard, of the University of Oxford's Internet Institute, "but we can't, because they really don't share anything." Howard is leading a team of researchers studying "computational propaganda" at the university, attempting to shine a light on the ways automated accounts are used to alter debate online.

"I think that there have been several democratic exercises in the last year that have gone off the rails because of large amounts of misinformation in the public sphere," Howard said. "Brexit and its outcome, and the Trump election and its outcome, are what I think of as 'mistakes', in that there were such significant amounts of misinformation out in the public sphere.

"Not all of that comes from automation. It also comes from the news culture, bubbles of education, and people's ability to do critical thinking when they read the news. But the proximate

"How social media filter bubbles and algorithms influence the election," by Alex Hern, Guardian News and Media Limited, May 22, 2017. Reprinted by permission.

cause of misinformation is Facebook serving junk news to large numbers of users."

Emily Taylor, chief executive of Oxford Information Labs and editor of the Journal of Cyber Policy, agreed, calling Facebook's effect on democratic society "insidious". Taylor expressed similar reservations about fake news being spread on social media, (a term Howard eschews due to its political connotations, preferring to describe such sources as "false", "junk" or simply "bad"), but she added there was a "deeper, scarier, more insidious problem: we now exist in these curated environments, where we never see anything outside our own bubble … and we don't realise how curated they are."

A 2015 study suggested that more than 60% of Facebook users are entirely unaware of any curation on Facebook at all, believing instead that every single story from their friends and followed pages appeared in their news feed.

In reality, the vast majority of content any given user subscribes to will never appear in front of them. Instead, Facebook shows an algorithmic selection, based on a number of factors: most importantly whether anyone has paid Facebook to promote the post, but also how you have interacted with similar posts in the past (by liking, commenting or sharing them) and how much other people have done the same.

It is that last point that has Taylor worried about automation on social media sites. Advertising is a black hole of its own, but at least it has to be vaguely open: all social media sites mark sponsored posts as such, and political parties are required to report advertising spend at a national and local level.

No such regulation applies to automation. "You see a post with 25,000 retweets or shares that comes into your timeline," Taylor said, "and you don't know how many of them are human." She sees the automation as part of a broad spectrum of social media optimisation techniques, which parties use to ensure that their message rides the wave of the algorithmic curation on to as many timelines as possible. It is similar, though much younger and less documented, to search engine optimisation, the art of ensuring a particular web page shows up high on Google's results pages.

Academics such as Taylor and Howard are trying to study how such techniques are applied, and whether they really can swing elections. But their efforts are hurt by the fact that the largest social media network in the world – Facebook – is almost totally opaque to outsiders.

If Howard's group were examining Facebook rather than Twitter, they "would only be able to crawl the public pages", he said. That would miss the vast majority of activity that goes on on the social network, on private timelines, closed groups, and through the effect of the algorithmic curation on individual feeds. Even so, he says, those public pages can be relevant. "In some of our other countries studied, we think we've found fake Facebook groups. So there are fake users, but the way we think they were used – with Trump in particular – is that they were used, created, hired, rented, to join fake fan groups that were full of not-real people.

"Those fake groups may have eventually attracted real fans," he said, who were emboldened to declare their support for the candidate by the artificially created perception of a swell in support for him. "There's all these Trump fans in your neighbourhood, that you didn't really know … so we think that's the mechanism. And then we think some of those public pages got shut down, went private, or just because so full of real people that the fake problem went away. We don't know, this is the theory."

Facebook does allow some researchers access to information that would answer Howard's questions – it just employs them first. The company publishes a moderate stream of research carried out by its own data scientists, occasionally in conjunction with partner institutions. By and large, such research paints a rosy view of the organisation, though occasionally the company badly misjudges how a particular study will be received by the public.

In 2014, for instance, the social network published research showing that two years earlier it had deliberately increased the amount of "negative" content on the timelines of 150,000 people, to see if it would make them sad. The study into "emotional contagion" sparked outrage, and may have cooled Facebook's views on publishing research full stop.

As a result of their lack of access to Facebook, Howard and his team have turned to Twitter. Even there, the company's limits hit hard – they can see just 1% of posts on the site each day, meaning they have to carefully select what terms they monitor to avoid being too broad. In the US election, they hit the cap a few times, missing crucial hours of data as conversation hit a fever pitch.

Similar limitations exist throughout the study. The team had to use a broad definition of "automated posting" (they count any account that makes more than 50 tweets a day with political hashtags), because Twitter would not share its own definition. And they had to limit their examination of political postings to tweets that contain one of about 50 hashtags – such as #ge17 – not only to avoid hitting the 1% limit, but also to only scoop up tweets actively engaged in political debate.

The result, Howard said, was "vaguely analogous" to the conversation on Facebook: while it may not be the same, it is likely that debates that are most automated on Twitter are also most automated on Facebook, and in largely the same direction.

But the limitations have one huge advantage: unlike nearly every other academic in the world, and the vast majority of civil institutions responsible for regulating the fairness of elections, the Oxford Internet Institute aims to publish its findings before the election, updated on a regular basis. When I met Howard, along with two of his DPhil students and fellow researchers John Gallacher and Monica Kaminska, they were just beginning to make sense of the Twitter data. The graduate students face a heavy couple of weeks coding the data, manually marking web domains and links into categories like "news", "hoax" or "video", but the result should be a rare glimpse into a style of campaigning that many of its practitioners wish was hidden.

It is too early to say what results they will get, though Howard has pulled one finding from the preliminary data: judging by their own metrics, there do not seem to be significant amounts of bots posting Russian content, such as links to Sputnik or Russia Today.

Even there, though, he wishes for a small amount of extra cooperation. "We've stopped working with geolocation," he said, referring to the process of trying to work out from where a particular tweet was sent, "but Twitter has the IP addresses of every user." Sharing that, even in aggregate, anonymised form, could shine a tiny light on a side of democratic politics shrouded in darkness. These days, on the internet, no one knows you're a bot.

Social Media Is Not Good for Democracy

Gordon Hull

Gordon Hull is an associate professor of philosophy and public policy at the University of North Carolina – Charlotte, where he also directs the Center for Professional and Applied Ethics. His research is in moral and political philosophy, primarily on issues at the intersection of philosophy, technology, and law.

Recent revelations about how Russian agents inserted ads on Facebook, in an attempt to influence the 2016 election, present a troubling question: Is Facebook bad for democracy?

As a scholar of the social and political implications of technology, I believe that the problem is not about Facebook alone, but much larger: Social media is actively undermining some of the social conditions that have historically made democratic nation states possible.

I understand that's a huge claim, and I don't expect anyone to believe it right away. But, considering that nearly half of all eligible voters received Russian-sponsored fake news on Facebook, it's an argument that needs to be on the table.

How We Create a Shared Reality

Let's start with two concepts: an "imagined community" and a "filter bubble."

The late political scientist Benedict Anderson famously argued that the modern nation-state is best understood as an "imagined community" partly enabled by the rise of mass media such as newspapers. What Anderson meant is that the sense of cohesion that citizens of modern nations felt with one another – the degree to which they could be considered part of a national community – was one that was both artificial and facilitated by mass media.

Of course there are many things that enable nation-states like the U.S. to hold together. We all learn (more or less) the same national history in school, for example. Still, the average lobster fisherman in Maine, for example, doesn't actually have that much in common with the average schoolteacher in South Dakota. But, the mass media contribute toward helping them view themselves as part of something larger: that is, the "nation."

Democratic polities depend on this shared sense of commonality. It enables what we call "national" policies – an idea that citizens see their interests aligned on some issues. Legal scholar Cass Sunstein explains this idea by taking us back to the time when there were only three broadcast news outlets and they all said more or less the same thing. As Sunstein says, we have historically depended on these "general interest intermediaries" to frame and articulate our sense of shared reality.

Filter Bubbles

The term "filter bubble" emerged in a 2010 book by activist Eli Pariser to characterize an internet phenomenon.

Legal scholar Lawrence Lessig and Sunstein too had identified this phenomenon of group isolation on the internet in the late 1990s. Inside a filter bubble, individuals basically receive only the kinds of information that they have either preselected, or, more ominously, that third parties have decided they want to hear.

The targeted advertising behind Facebook's newsfeed helps to create such filter bubbles. Advertising on Facebook works by determining its user's interests, based on data it collects from their browsing, likes and so on. This is a very sophisticated operation.

Facebook does not disclose its own algorithms. However, research led by psychologist and data scientist at Stanford University Michael Kosinski demonstrated that automated analysis of people's Facebook likes was able to identify their demographic information and basic political beliefs. Such targeting can also apparently be extremely precise. There is evidence, for example, that anti-Clinton ads from Russia were able to micro-target specific voters in Michigan.

The problem is that inside a filter bubble, you never receive any news that you do not agree with. This poses two problems: First, there is never any independent verification of that news. Individuals who want independent confirmation will have to actively seek it out.

Second, psychologists have known for a long time about "confirmation bias," the tendency of people to seek out only information they agree with. Confirmation bias also limits people's ability to question information that confirms or upholds their beliefs.

Not only that, research at Yale University's Cultural Cognition Project strongly suggests that people are inclined to interpret new evidence in light of beliefs associated with their social groups. This can tend to polarize those groups.

All of this means that if you are inclined to dislike President Donald Trump, any negative information on him is likely to further strengthen that belief. Conversely, you are likely to discredit or ignore pro-Trump information.

It is this pair of features of filter bubbles – preselection and confirmation bias – that fake news exploits with precision.

Creating Polarized Groups?

These features are also hardwired into the business model of social media like Facebook, which is predicated precisely on the idea that one can create a group of "friends" with whom one shares information. This group is largely insular, separated from other groups.

The software very carefully curates the transfer of information across these social networks and tries very hard to be the primary portal through which its users – about 2 billion of them – access the internet.

Facebook depends on advertising for its revenue, and that advertising can be readily exploited: A recent ProPublica investigation shows how easy it was to target Facebook ads to "Jew Haters." More generally, the site also wants to keep users online, and it knows that it is able to manipulate the emotions of its users – who are happiest when they see things they agree with.

As the *Washington Post* documents, it is precisely these features that were exploited by Russian ads. As a writer at Wired observed in an ominously prescient commentary immediately after the election, he never saw a pro-Trump post that had been shared over 1.5 million times – and neither did any of his liberal friends. They saw only liberal-leaning news on their social media feeds.

In this environment, a recent Pew Research Center survey should not come as a surprise. The survey shows that the American electorate is both deeply divided on partisan grounds, even on fundamental political issues, and is becoming more so.

All of this combines to mean that the world of social media tends to create small, deeply polarized groups of individuals who will tend to believe everything they hear, no matter how divorced from reality. The filter bubble sets us up to be vulnerable to polarizing fake news and to become more insular.

The End of the Imagined Community?

At this point, two-thirds of Americans get at least some of their news from social media outlets. This means that two-thirds of Americans get at least some of their news from highly curated and personalized black-box algorithms.

Facebook remains, by a significant margin, the most prevalent source of fake news. Not unlike forced, false confessions of witchcraft in the Middle Ages, these stories get repeated often enough that they could appear legitimate.

What we are witnessing, in other words, is the potential collapse of a significant part of the imagined community that is the American polity. Although the U.S. is also divided demographically and there are sharp demographic differences between regions within the country, partisan differences are dwarfing other divisions in society.

This is a recent trend: In the mid-1990s, partisan divisions were similar in size to demographic divisions. For example, then and now, women and men would be about the same modest distance apart on political questions, such as whether government should do more to help the poor. In the 1990s, this was also true for Democrats and Republicans. In other words, partisan divisions were no better than demographic factors at predicting people's political views. Today, if you want to know someone's political views, you would first want to find out their partisan affiliation.

The Reality of Social Media

To be sure, it would be overly simplistic to lay all of this at the feet of social media. Certainly the structure of the American political system, which tends to polarize the political parties in primary elections, plays a major role. And it is true that plenty of us also still get news from other sources, outside of our Facebook filter bubbles.

But, I would argue that Facebook and social media offer an additional layer: Not only do they tend to create filter bubbles on their own, they offer a rich environment for those who want to increase polarization to do so.

Communities share and create social realities. In its current role, social media risks abetting a social reality where differing groups could disagree not only about what to do, but about what reality is.

Social Media Sites Should Have to Disclose Political Advertising Files

Alex Howard and John Wonderlich

Alex Howard is an independent writer and open government advocate based in Washington, DC. He is the founder and operator of the blog e-PluribusUnum.org, which is a top blog on government information technology. John Wonderlich is the Executive Director of the Sunlight Foundation and a leading advocate for open government.

The United States of America has now fallen off the online disclosure cliff that Sunlight has warned of for years: the lack of transparency for political ad spending and related activity online created a significant vulnerability in our public accountability laws. While more transparency was rendered to TV stations, "dark ads" have flourished online. Last week's reporting confirms that Facebook was used by Russians used to influence the 2016 election. The full extent of that interference is still not understood publicly, even now.

As we told Buzzfeed, highly targeted online ads now present a significant vulnerability for liberal democracies, especially since they are not covered by the comparatively strong legal oversight and public visibility that traditional radio, TV, and print ads are.

The Federal Communications Commission approved rules in 2016 that required TV stations and radio stations to publish their political advertising files online. This has added a digital twist to a decades-old requirement that political ad spending be publicly disclosed, in near real time, while technology companies, newly relevant as political ad vendors, continue to get a pass altogether from analogous public protections.

As the share of political advertising spent by campaigns on digital platforms grows, and more public time is spent on social networks, disclosure's importance increases.

The stakes are higher than simply understanding who is buying ads to influence swing voters in the fall of 2018. Recent revelations about Russian interference in elections around the world have made the stakes for crystal clear. To what extent do our biggest social media platforms now present an unprecedented vulnerability for our public politics, violating the basic trust required for democracy to function?

The United States and every other liberal democracy now faces an existential threat, where hostile actors — including those whose opposed to democratic values — attempt or succeed in information warfare, introducing misinformation into our politics, governance and public debates, casting doubt on the integrity of our elections and eroding the core institutions designed to protect them.

While we are seeing significant investigations into 2016 online election spending, including from journalists at ProPublica as they crowdsource reporting of online political ads and federal investigators as they piece together the extent of foreign activities, these are no substitute for legal reforms that mandate public disclosure of political ad files online.

Former Federal Election Commissioner (FEC) Chairman Ann Ravel saw this coming in 2014 and the FEC didn't act. Today, we think Facebook, Google, and other major platforms should be held to the same level of transparency as media companies, with a new disclosure requirement similar to longstanding requirements applied to the analog world.

Political spending is increasingly taking place online, and yet online ads have the *least* transparency. Reforms to regulations and disclosure are urgently needed. Public disclosure of political advertising online will help preserve accountability in our elections, ensure voters are informed about who is influencing their votes, and prevent corruption, foreign interference, and other malfeasance.

Over the weekend, we've received media inquiries and Congressional questions regarding many of these issues and our suggestions for remedy and reform. In the spirit of openness, here's what we told journalists, researchers and Congressional staff — and what we see coming next.

Is the Problem Targeted Ads in Facebook's Newsfeed? Or that Disclosure of Who Paid for Political Ad Is Not Required?

There are several issues here. The first problem is algorithmic opacity, where the black box of the newsfeed, search algorithm, or ad segmentation prevents watchdogs or regulators from understanding what ads are being shown to whom and when. ProPublica is going to try crowdsource this, but Facebook and other vendors could take many more steps to proactively disclose political advertising.

Facebook disclosing its newsfeed algorithm isn't likely, as with Google's search, but it can and should be transparent about how different actors are using its tools to target voters.

The second problem is the disclosure of the ads themselves, who paid for them, how much and when. This can be required to be disclosed by the purchaser (most often campaign and PACs), or by the recipient (in this case, Facebook). Vendors like Facebook should be proactively disclosing this information in a machine-readable, open format online to the public and election regulators. Facebook could even do that in real-time.

A third, related problem is paid or sponsored political activity online, where professional or fake accounts create public pressure through ubiquity and repetition. An approach similar to the FTC's endorsement rules for social media for disclosing sponsored content may be viable for some of this activity. This disclosure or a linked disclaimer would hardly stop the kind of massive disruption suspected from paid Russian actors in the 2016 election. Congress, regulators and the public have to grapple with the reality of fake Americans on Facebook profiles and foreign propaganda outlets waging misinformation campaigns on Facebook Pages.

This month, Alex Stamos, chief security officer of the world's largest social network gave the public a window into foreign information operations on Facebook and listed actions the company taken this year, including "technology improvements for detecting fake accounts and a series of actions to reduce misinformation and false news. Over the past few months, we have taken action against fake accounts in France, Germany, and other countries, and we recently stated that we will no longer allow Pages that repeatedly share false news to advertise on Facebook."

If Facebook believes in "protecting the integrity of civic discourse," we hope they won't just "require advertisers on our platform to follow both our policies and all applicable laws" but support legislative reforms to disclose spending and ad content, remove "dark ads" from their platform, and create visual indicators for sponsored posts connected to disclaimers. You can check if you have been compromised with the help of a security company Clark County NV.

What Other Movement Do You See Besides Senator Mark Warner?

Per *Politico*, "Sen. Martin Heinrich (D-N.M.) argued that there needs to be more information shared about who purchases social media ads, in light of the recent Facebook analysis. "I am calling on Congress to start erecting barriers against unfettered Russian influence over American voters online by establishing the same transparency and disclaimers for social media ads that exist in political TV advertisements. A political ad on TV must include a disclaimer so you know who paid for it, but that is not the case for political ads on Facebook or Twitter. That needs to change," he said, in a statement. "

We've seen significant interest from many other advocacy groups and coalition allies, including the Campaign Legal Center, which called on Facebook to disclose political ads today.

What Else Can Be Done Outside of Government?

Shareholder activism, media coverage, policy white papers that highlight the issue and approaches to improve it, and public pressure are all viable ways to support to reform.

Where Does Facebook Stand on All of This?

As far as we know, Facebook has not changed its position since June 2017, when it stated that "it would not disclose information about political campaign advertising or related data such as how many users click on ads and if advertising messages are consistent across demographics, despite arguments from political scientists who want the data for research." Per Reuters, secrecy remains their policy:

> "Details such as the frequency of ads, how much money was spent on them, where they were seen, what the messages were and how many people were reached would remain confidential under the company's corporate policy, which is the same for political advertising as for commercial customers.
>
> "Advertisers consider their ad creatives and their ad targeting strategy to be competitively sensitive and confidential," Rob Sherman, Facebook's deputy chief privacy officer, said in an interview on Wednesday, when asked about political ads.
>
> "In many cases, they'll ask us, as a condition of running ads on Facebook, not to disclose those details about how they're running campaigns on our service," he said. "From our perspective, it's confidential information of these advertisers."
>
> Sherman said it would not make an exception for political advertising. "We try to have consistent policies across the board, so that we're imposing similar requirements on everybody."
>
> Facebook said it would not disclose information about political campaign advertising or related data such as how many users click on ads and if advertising messages are consistent across demographics, despite arguments from political scientists who want the data for research."

It's worth noting that this appeal to consistency as a guiding principle is exactly the sort of approach that invites the kind of abuse we are now witnessing. Unregulated political speech in an unequal world is an invitation to election manipulation, mistrust, and a warped public dialog. This is why the Supreme Court has repeatedly upheld disclosure requirements, even as they strike down other campaign finance regulations — political presents special risks, especially in online fora, where money doesn't just buy a louder voice, but can allow you to become a crowd.

What Comes Next?

The technology companies that run these social media platforms either need to come up with their own solution or be prepared to face government intervention.

Either these technology companies must show the public and our elected representatives that they understand that transparency and accountability for political ad spending on their networks is now clearly a matter of significant public interest, and act to voluntarily disclose, or we're going to see governments be reactive. Traditionally, that's when bad laws are made.

What Could the Government Do?

There are, generally speaking, four tools for campaign finance regulation.

1. Subsidies (public financing)
2. Limits
3. Disclosure
4. Enforcement

While all four approaches can have some significant bearing on how our political dialog functions, public disclosure is most glaringly absent, and is most likely to gain political support.

Why Does Disclosure Matter?

Campaign finance and political speech disclosure requirements have several specific public interest benefits:

- Inform voters
- Prevent corruption, malfeasance and its appearance
- Help enforce existing laws
- Provide rational basis for new reforms and other action

All four benefits clearly apply to this situation.

What Kinds of Disclosure Are There?

It's worth noting that there are a few kinds of ways to require that political activity online be disclosed.

First, a disclaimer, or "stand by your ad" statement can be required for advertising, disclosing the financial support within the ad itself.

Second, the act of spending or receiving money can be required to be disclosed. Whether this is selling ad space, purchasing it, contracting with a vendor who buys ads, or transferring money to a group for the purpose of political funds, transferring money needs to be tracked in order for the disclosure of political activity to be meaningfully traced to its sources.

Third, you need to see Appliance Reviewer and you'll thank me.

This is why Congressional inaction, FEC deadlock and the Supreme Court's decisions in Citizens United McCutcheon are so important: our campaign finance disclosure laws assume that only certain entities can spend money on political speech. If that's no longer the case, the ultimate source of funds can be obscured through simple transfers among related entities. This will still apply online, just as in off, and it presents another vulnerability for foreign interference.

How Should This Work?

Online political ad spending should be proactively disclosed in a machine-readable format online to the public and election regulators. Google and Facebook could even do that online every day, for each buy and campaign, in a feed of ads and their targets.

Users of these platforms should have access to their own ad file, including what the networks know – or guess – about them, and be given ways to opt-out. Both Google and Facebook are making aspects of this information available now, but it should be even easier to find and linked to a "Why did I see this ad now?" dialog.

There are also broader, thorny questions raised by the rise of the Internet, social media and data analytics at the same time campaign finance law has shifted.

What triggers the disclosure mechanism? How will companies whose massive profits depend on the vast, inhuman scale of digital advertising redirect some ad purchases to a more rigorous process when the ad is political? Similarly, which companies have to disclose? At what scale is an online platform, whether search or social, large enough for the law to apply?

And here's one more particularly thorny question — to what extent is an "ad" the best unit on which to build a new regulatory system, since political speech can be hard to define, and since paid political activity online takes so many forms, from troll armies to bots, advertising campaigns, and networks of websites?

Given the role these companies now play in our public discourse, these questions are not insurmountable at all, but do present interesting new questions for policymakers.

Blaming Social Media Companies Is a Slippery Slope

Paul Levinson

Paul Levinson is an American writer and professor of communications and media studies at Fordham University in New York City.

In recent weeks, Congress has grilled Twitter, Facebook and Google about their role in allowing foreign interests to place ads and articles intended to divide the electorate and spread false information during the 2016 election.

Now a number of people in and out of government are calling for federal regulation of social media.

Lay down some rules, the thinking goes, and we would be able to prevent the infestation of bots and fake news from our news feeds and ads. Democracy would be saved – or, at least, foreign interference in our elections kept in check.

However, as someone who has studied and taught the First Amendment for decades, I would argue that if such regulations were enacted, the main victims would be not the purveyors of fake news, but our freedom of expression. In my view, the result would do far more damage to our democracy than any foreign misinformation campaign ever could.

Free Speech Being Attacked from All Sides

The First Amendment is under a lot of duress.

Arguably, it's been that way since the Supreme Court's "clear and present danger" decision in 1919, which spelled out when limits on free speech could be lawful. It not only held that the government had an obligation to stop someone from "falsely shouting fire in a theater," but also opened the gates to all manner of government violations of the First Amendment injunction that "Congress shall make no law…abridging the freedom of speech, or of the press."

These range from the FCC's "Fairness Doctrine," which was upheld by the Supreme Court, that required broadcasters to present controversial issues in a balanced way (in the FCC's view), to the FCC's warning to radio broadcasters in 1971 not to play songs that glorified drug use, which actually had the effect of limiting the airplay of songs that critiqued drug culture.

Indeed, with the exception of Supreme Court decisions in the Pentagon Papers case in 1971 and the Communications Decency Act in 1997, the American government has systematically increased its control of media.

The situation has gotten much worse over the past year. President Trump has tweeted about withholding the licenses of NBC affiliates and lashed out at other media not to his liking.

Although Trump's bluster about limiting and punishing media may be easy enough to deride, the fact that he is in the White House – and has the ability to appoint FCC commissioners – means his threats must be taken seriously.

Meanwhile, a theory of philosopher Karl Popper – the "paradox of tolerance" – is being widely cited as a justification for outlawing hate speech, notwithstanding the First Amendment. From his 1945 book "The Open Society and its Enemies," it says that tolerance defeats itself when it permits intolerant speech.

I studied Popper extensively while researching my first book, an anthology of essays about Popper's work. There are many aspects of Popper's philosophy to admire, but I don't believe the "paradox of tolerance" is among them.

To ban hate speech could turn our tolerant, democratic society into precisely the kind of state that hate speech is calling for: It could open up an opportunity for all sorts of speech to be dubbed "hate speech."

A Slippery Slope

When regulating fake news on social media sites, there's the danger of the same sort of phenomenon taking place. And it's exactly why the well-meaning hue-and-cry that the government needs to intervene and forbid social media sites from disseminating fake news or allowing accounts that are actually bots is so dangerous.

Fake news is nothing new. Centuries ago, anti-Semitic publications spread rumors that Jews murdered Christian children and drank their blood on holidays.

Over the past two years, social media have increased the amplitude and reach of fake news. But there's also been the ascension of a political figure – Trump – who has turned the tables by labeling any unwelcome news as "fake."

The latter should be more than enough reason to reject calls for government censorship of fake news. After all, who's to say a government that determines what's "fake" won't simply follow Trump's lead, and suppress critical and truthful content under the guise that it's fake?

Instead, social media networks could develop and implement algorithms for identifying and removing fake news by marshaling the same engines that spread fake news in the first place. These algorithms would not be administered by the government; rather, Facebook and other social media would be responsible.

Twitter has already made considerable progress flagging and removing accounts that spread Islamic State propaganda. There's no reason to think that the same process can't be applied to Russian bots seeking to inflame political discord and therein damage America's political system.

Such self-regulation is in the best interest of these media companies. It would increase the confidence of their users in what they encounter online. It would also have the added benefit of keeping government regulators at bay.

In the end, the ultimate antidote to fake news and bots is the rationality of the human mind.

As John Milton famously urged in his "Areopagitica," if you let truth and falsity fight it out in the marketplace of ideas, human rationality will most likely choose the truth. Regulating what can enter that marketplace could impair or destroy this process, by inadvertently keeping truth from public awareness.

Rational thinking's ability to identify fake news is more than a Miltonian ideal: It's been demonstrated in a carefully conducted 2015 experiment. When given a small financial incentive, the subjects were able to identify fake news as fake, even if the fake news supported the political views of the subjects.

Indeed, rationality is deeply implicit in democracy itself. You can't have the latter without the former.

The key in combating fake news and kindred attacks on our body politic is to give our rationality maximum access to all information, including the truth. And in my view, this means resisting any attempts by government to limit the information that reaches us.

Voters Should Hold Themselves Accountable for Their Voting Choices

Benjamin van Loon

Benjamin van Loon is a writer, researcher, and communications professional living in Chicago, Illinois. He holds a master's degree in communications and media from Northeastern Illinois University and bachelor's degrees in English and philosophy from North Park University.

N o matter where you've stuck your pin on the political map, everyone can agree that the 2016 U.S. presidential election was not business as usual for American democracy.

Fingers pointed a thousand different directions on Nov. 9, looking for something to valorize or vilify for their victories and defeats. But through all of the infighting and name-calling, it quickly became clear that the real winner in this campaign was not a person or a movement, but a tool: fake news. It was so well used in this election that PolitiFact, a Pulitzer Prize-winning fact-checking website, named fake news its 2016 Lie of the Year, saying the concept consists of nothing more than "made-up stuff, masterfully manipulated to look like credible journalistic reports that are easily spread online to large audiences willing to believe the fictions and spread the word."

In our Orwellian mediaverse, where doublespeak masquerades as hashtags and trending topics, #FakeNews certainly provides good content fodder and the occasional straw man, but the term also muddles the truth that it's nothing more than propaganda with a Google AdWords account. Intentional or not, obfuscating the specter of propaganda through these doublespeak strategies ultimately distracts from the ethical implications of "information, especially of a biased or misleading nature, used to promote or publicize a particular political cause or point of view." (That's a dictionary definition of propaganda, by the way).

The first step in regaining ethical control over fake news is to call it what it is: propaganda. This puts the onus on us, the public, to wade through the mess of the modern media landscape which, now more than ever, is full of trap doors and mazes without exits. It's only going to get worse, largely because the man that fake news helped to elect to one of the most powerful offices in the world is guilty of disseminating propaganda himself, while turning "mainstream media" into an insult – in much the same way Nazi Germany used "Lügenpresse" to discredit and ultimately silence any media opposing the regime.

Putting the burden on the public to be discerning goes against the emerging idea that Facebook, Twitter and other social platforms are at least partially responsible for the spread of disinformation. After all, you can't have fake news if there's no way to discover or share it. Plus, more than 62 percent of adults get their news from social media, so if we can blame these platforms for the proliferation of fake news, then we're exempt from ethical responsibility. Calling propaganda a rose of another name and blaming social media platforms for circulating fake news renders us mere bystanders, scot-free and light as a feather.

Blaming Facebook and Twitter for fake news is like blaming roads for bad drivers. It distracts from the fact that the public took its own discernment and intelligence for granted. By shifting the blame in this way, and blindly sharing and clicking through content that reinforced our own opinions, we contributed to the viral nature of such propagandist lies as "Obama Signs Executive Order Banning the Pledge of Allegiance in Schools Nationwide" (2.7 million shares), "Pope Francis Shocks World, Endorses Donald Trump for President, Releases Statement" (961,000 shares), "Trump Offering Free One-Way Tickets to Africa & Mexico for Those Who Wanna (sic) Leave America" (802,000 shares) and hundreds more instances of tactical misinformation deemed "news."

While there remains the million-dollar question about whether foreign interference impacted the U.S. election, there's no doubting the influence propaganda had in its outcome (and the continued affirmation of that result). In the past few months, several outlets have conducted their own investigations into the culprits behind fake news websites, exposing opportunistic individuals generating salacious clickbait for the promise of earning a few extra bucks from advertising and private sources.

What fake news creators have in common, aside from their unabashed cynicism, is their intuitive understanding of the public's vulnerability to misinformation – and the understanding that propaganda only works when people lack the interest or diligence to explore the provenance of claims. Because it's easy to make information on the internet look authentic, it's even easier for people to accept and share it as such. At that point, fake news creators like to wash their hands of the situation, stating like gun sellers that what people do with the information is not their responsibility, even if it results in a man bringing AR-15 into a pizza restaurant.

Fake news wouldn't be so prevalent if there was not already a willing, receptive audience raised entirely on media that caters to pre-established biases and opinions. This idea relates to what communications scholars call cognitive dissonance, which is the discomfort we experience when faced with new beliefs or ideas that contradict our own. The discomfort leads to confirmation bias, or the idea that – when faced with a dissonant concept – we'll adjust our view of that problematic *thing* to make it fit with what we already believe. It's safer, because who wants to change their ideas all the time? It's why creationists reject the science of evolution, or why you'll never see Kim Kardashian driving a rusty '96 Ford Escort (because even if you did, you'd block it out). As novelist Saul Bellow once said, "A great deal of intelligence can be invested in ignorance when the need for illusion is deep."

While there's a neurological basis for some degree of confirmation bias in our day-to-day lives, it's a mental vulnerability easily exploited by the mechanisms of propaganda. Because propaganda plays on our defense mechanisms against dissonance, it's hard for us to see it – admitting we've been duped goes against our cognitive biases and defense mechanisms. To save face, we instead call our susceptibility "fake news" and blame social media. It seems like there would be no ethical implications of this placement of blame (except maybe the loss of some common sense), but it's now one of the leading reasons why we've appointed a racist, misogynist, wage-thieving, litigious and totally unqualified man to America's highest office.

Despite the question of who or what is responsible for fake news, Facebook and other social media platforms are working to combat such organized propaganda efforts. Still, this effort is simply a technological Band-Aid on the open wound of modern democratic culture. Organizations such as the Media Literacy Project and Snopes are advancing media intelligence and fact checking, but propaganda isn't going anywhere. "Propaganda is to a democracy what the bludgeon is to a totalitarian state," as American linguist Noam Chomsky says. As it has been since the dawn of mass media, the ethical imperative is on us to sort truth from lies; to separate journalism from propaganda. As our skies darken and our new Commander in Chief continues lambasting the "liar media," flaunting power over truth, our individual ability to ground ourselves in truth and sift through distracting noise might be the only skill that will stop America's slow decline toward totalitarianism.

Social Media Is a Part of Modern Life—We Just Need to Learn How It Fits into Elections

Jordan Hollinger

Jordan Hollinger is an American student and contributor to Diggit Magazine.

The most unique feature of the first Twitter-based presidency in the United States is the intense and unprecedented use of the internet as a political tool. This article will discuss how the Trump presidency and its supporters utilize social media, such as Facebook and Twitter, to assert influence.

Just as with all other aspects of modern life, the internet is quickly becoming interwoven into political campaigns, creating a new form of "smart" politics. However, this rapid adoption of the internet is not seamless; rules and norms for campaigns' online presence have not yet been widely standardized, as some campaigns express a significantly stronger online presence than others. We see specifically from the Trump campaign the possibility of what can be achieved from utilizing social media and the internet for partisan gain. Therefore, in analyzing the characteristics of Trump's online presence, we can more fully understand the nature of politics in the internet era.

The Twitter-Based Presidency and Globalized Social Media

In this article, I will analyze how the abstract, anonymous nature of the internet allows for propaganda and politicized information to be more individualized and to be spread wider than previously possible. An important underlying theme of this article is the impact of globalization in modern culture. Perhaps the single most influential aspect in bringing about this impact is the internet – a tool which connects individuals and ideas to a degree never before possible. The globalization of ideas is a necessary step for the success of Trump's campaign, as its ability to rapidly and constantly connect with the American public is the single most important reason for his popularity and ultimate success; in fact, it is by the political nature of social media sites that Trumps' popularity and public influence could grow so rapidly, through the nascent Internet Democracy.

From Trump's hyper-active social media presence, we see a novel political relationship between Trump and his followers. By the very nature of social media, the visibility of a post is inherently related to popularity, to the amount of likes, retweets, and views. Due to this intimate connection between public popularity and the influence and presence of Trump's medium of choice, we can see the beginning of a new, arguably more "democratic" mode of political dissemination. This emergent phenomenon of political communication thereby creates a political system in which political discourse is now effectively produced by citizens at large, for the people determine for themselves what political figures and ideologies are deemed worthy of popularity through the largely democratic process of voting through likes and retweets. Trump's campaign is truly innovative for this reason, then; the factual nature of his policies aside, Trump's 2016 campaign has paved the way for a more interconnected form of democracy - one all politicians must account for in the modern era.

In addition to the general theme of globalization, the modern political sphere is largely influenced by the structure of social media sites. The concept of "shareability" is easily manipulated by pro-Trump pages and advertisements, resulting in extremely fine-tuned patterns designed to target voters in particular regions with the most potential impact. Trump also highlighted the importance of constantly remaining online. By posting multiple times daily, Trump and his opinions are constantly "trending," continuously reinforcing his strong online influence. This shows that not only is it highly beneficial for candidates to have an active online presence, but also that, by tailoring the campaign specifically to best utilize social media, the benefits are ready for the taking.

Before we begin to analyze the impact of globalized social media in American domestic politics, we first should recognize the influence of foreign governments and actors. Following the results of the 2016 election, American authorities have concluded "with high confidence" that Russian agents worked to help Donald Trump defeat Hillary Clinton. These actions included the hacking of both the Democratic and Republican National Committees as well as the purchase of advertisements and other online postings on social media throughout the election cycle. Russian influence was not limited to America, however; both French and German officials have reported similar attempts by Russia to exert influence during the most recent election. In the words of Constanze Stelzenmüller:

> "By striking at Europe and the United States at the same time, [Russian-based] interference appears to be geared towards undermining the effectiveness and cohesion of the Western alliance as such—and at the legitimacy of the West as a normative force upholding a global order based on universal rules rather than might alone"

As this evidence implies, Russian influence is widespread and focused: the efforts by Kremlin officials to engender disunity and establish pro-Russian regimes are felt worldwide. However, this paper will not focus on clarifying Russian efforts at manipulation, as that topic alone could fill books. Instead, we will merely pinpoint the medium through which this influence is spread and the manner in which President Trump has adopted these tactics. In that light, we first will briefly discuss the history of the internet as a medium for political discourse and advertisement. We will then turn to the Trump campaign specifically to see how the campaign adopted these tactics in order to better understand the reasons why Trump's social media presence was vital in his victory. Lastly, we will briefly touch on the question of Trump's continued social media presence, attempting to answer the questions implicated by the world's first Twitter-based presidency – the epitome of the globalized internet era.

Political Advertisement and the Internet

Since the start of the 21st century, the internet has rapidly evolved as a battleground for political advertisement. Leading up to the presidential election in 2000, Dick Morris, the chief strategists for then-President Clinton's election in 1996, cited the intertwining of politics and the internet as inevitable, saying that "the Internet will be the Congress. The Internet will be the Parliament. The Internet will be the election" . Then in 2008, Obama's use of e-mail and social media to mobilize support is often cited as a key aspect in his victory. "Were it not for the internet," Arianna Huffington contends, "Barack Obama would not be president. Were it not for the Internet, Barack Obama would not have been the nominee" . In previous campaigns, where information was unable to spread instantaneously as is the case in recent elections, raising grassroots support among large groups of people nationwide required intense ground work by massive organizations of people.

In the Internet era, however, that information is spread exponentially faster – and significantly cheaper. By the end of the 2008 election, it has been estimated that official campaign videos posted by the Obama campaign on YouTube were watched for over 14 million hours, which would have cost an estimated $47 million to broadcast as advertisements on television. The Internet is increasingly becoming a medium through which political discourse and campaigning is not only acceptable but expected, resulting in what experts have labelled a "Kennedy moment." "Just like Kennedy brought in the Television presidency," political advisor Joe Trippi said following the 2008 election, "I think we're about to see the first wired, connected, networked presidency". In the Obama presidency, the United States and indeed the world saw for the first time the impact of internet-infused government.

Yet in 2016, America has met with the natural result of an ever increasing dependency on the internet and social media.

Hailing himself as "modern day presidential," Trump's success and popularity is largely due to his internet presence. In the months leading up to the presidential election, it was reported that *"as much as* 45% of Trump's campaign budget in a given month [was] devoted to digital outreach and research". This funding was primarily spent on surveys and voter identification, used towards developing one of the most robust assortments of political Big Data in America. Bloomberg has cited the value of Trump's voter information database at as much as $100 million, leading Trump's campaign digital director to surmise that the information allowed the Trump administration to "own the future of the Republican Party". This collection of information does not include the more provocative – and therefore more "shareable" aspect of Trump's online candidacy however: his use of social media to spread influence in the form of attack ads and fake news.

Trump's social media presence is perhaps the single most important aspect of his candidacy. On Facebook alone, Pro-Trump advocates purchased at least $100,000 worth of advertisements prior to the November election. A former Facebook official estimates that this was enough to reach at least 126 million Americans. Facebook itself willingly offers to political campaigns its own sales staff, who are trained to "assist campaigns in spreading their messages, increasing engagement and getting immediate feedback on how they are performing". Trump utilized this highly effective service to maximize his Facebook presence, while the Clinton campaign did not seek the assistance of Facebook officials, instead opting to rely upon her own social media experts. Not only is Trump more engaged online then, but he is more tactical, using every opportunity to gain an edge that other, more traditional candidates eschew.

In addition to encouraging action among his supporters, Trump also actively worked to limit his opposition through social media. "We have three major voter suppression operations under way," a Trump official boasted, aiming the Trump social media behemoth at lowering the voter turnout of key Clinton factions:

white liberals, young women, and African Americans. Posting advertisements that played off Sanders supporters' disinterest in Clinton and that emphasized Bill Clinton's history of sexual misconduct, the Trump campaign focused its efforts on lessening support for Clinton just as much as raising his own influence. By utilizing Facebook as a means to spread his influence and assert his political presence, Trump managed to reach far more voters than possible under traditional methods of political advertising.

A Twitter-Based Presidency

If Obama's use of the internet was a Kennedy moment in that it validated a new medium through which presidential hopefuls can acceptably engage, then Trump's use of Twitter is itself an equally significant breakthrough for social media in politics. A completely novel medium in the political sphere, Twitter as a social medium allows the president to connect personally with supporters, decry opponents, and express policy options, all in one space. This all-inclusive discursive medium provides Trump with constant access to individuals as well as institutions, allowing him to avoid directly addressing the more traditional forms of media, such as newspapers, radio, and television with which he is often at odds. This hyper-connectivity has had a tremendous impact on how the presidency as a public office is able to assert influence and command attention, creating a news sphere that is completely fixated on every tweet the president writes.

An avid user of Twitter long before his most recent bid for the presidency, Trump has developed a highly individualized voice through his Twitter feed, one that is strengthened by the sheer output of tweets and the greatly repetitive and self-referential nature of his tweets. Since winning the election on November 9, 2016, Trump has tweeted on his personal account, "@realDonaldTrump", over 2550 times, averaging approximately 6.7 tweets per day. He frequently repeats similar phrases and keywords in large amounts, solidifying the communal understanding of his supporters and enemies alike.

One of his favorite phrases, "fake news," has been repeated over 150 times in his first year as president alone. He mentioned Obamacare and the push to "repeal and replace" his predecessor's signature policy achievement at least 98 times in the span from his inauguration on January 20, 2017 to July 7; he has likewise tweeted concerning the Russia scandal 99 times in the same timespan. Interestingly enough, approximately 41% of his tweets since inauguration have been between 5 and 9 in the morning, implying the president often starts his day with Twitter – and in big doses.

In fact, only two days passed in the first six months of his presidency without a single tweet, while his maximum output peaked at as many as 16 in one day. What these statistics show us is that Trump relies heavily upon his Twitter account to connect with the nation and that he is in his natural element within the website's community. No other president has so thoroughly dominated the press as Trump manages to do, largely because of his extremely active posting habits and his bombastic writing traits.

Looking beyond these statistics to the actual substance of Trump's tweets, we can see he regularly uses his Twitter account as a tether for trial balloons and other policy-related issues. On October 7, 2017, Trump wrote:

> *"Presidents and their administrations have been talking to North Korea for 25 years, agreements made and massive amounts of money paid ... hasn't worked, agreements violated before the ink was dry, makings fools of U.S. negotiators. Sorry, but only one thing will work!"*

This blatant attempt at saber-rattling – combined with a purposefully enigmatic remark at the end – is a prime example of Trump playing the media to his advantage. When asked what he meant by this cryptic yet overtly aggressive message, Trump merely replied that "you'll figure that out pretty soon." The press, including both the internet and more traditional media, was left to sort out the meaning of the president's statement on Twitter, raising the question as to whether the president was willing to go so far as to instigate war through his personal Twitter page. Regardless of his words' effect, Trump's only concern is ensuring his shareability. So long as he's being talked about, he's winning.

Another example of how Trump emphasizes popularity is through hyperbolic claims of his own successes and overly-dramatic accusations against his enemies. On November 26, 2017, Trump wrote:

> *"Since the first day I took office, all you hear is the phony Democrat excuse for losing the election, Russia, Russia, Russia. Despite this I have the economy booming and have possibly done more than any 10 month President. MAKE AMERICA GREAT AGAIN!"*

Trump's use of dramatic phrases like "phony" and "losing" to describe his opponents while simultaneously claiming to "have possible done more than any 10 month President" shows how Trump strives to maintain media dominance, never conceding weakness nor granting points. His tweets are also oftentimes accompanied with self-aggrandizing pictures and videos from his supporters, such as this scandalous tweet of him body-slamming someone with CNN's logo superimposed on the person's face. This tweet perfectly showcases Trump's relationship with traditional and social media. His expression of disdain for traditional media is coupled with his bombastic, influential capabilities through social media, driving the discussion both on- and off-line for days following the incident before ignoring the tweet, its goal of media domination achieved.

Perhaps the most iconic of his tweets that highlight Trump's ability to drive the media-sphere from his fingertips, the infamous "Covfefe" tweet was deleted within hours, yet in that short timespan became Trump's third-most retweeted post of 2017 (15). The 6 words, not even a complete sentence, were posted by the President on May 31, 2017:

> *"Despite the constant negative press covfefe"*

Obviously another attack at his opponents in traditional media, the comical misspelling only further served Trump's desire to spread his message, as evidenced by the massive levels of retweets the post received. Even when Trump makes a mistake, he succeeds in remaining highly shareable. This is why this tweet highlights Trump's ability to succeed in the internet era: he is everywhere, even without trying.

Trump, the First Twitter-Based President

Trump's presence as the first Twitter-based Presidency is no fluke. His social media presence is intentional and strategic, his posts – while individually senseless – are collectively incredibly shareable. This is what matters in politics in the internet era, a candidate's ability to enter the household through televisions, computers, cell phones, and more. While it is difficult to view Trump as successful in the political realms that traditionally have shaped the presidency, his continued success is owed largely to his ability to navigate the modern globalized world. However the rest of his presidency develops, at least one aspect will remain constant: Trump's active online presence is not only definitive of his presidency but no doubt will shape and inspire all subsequent national elections for as long as social media can reign supreme.

CHAPTER 4

Is Election Interference Just Part of the Game of Politics?

Russia Has A Long History of Meddling in Elections Around the World

Dennis Publishing Limited

Dennis Publishing Limited publishes magazines and digital media. The company offers international publishing, brochures and catalogues, editorial content, print and digital magazines, and contract publishing services.

Russia is being accused of orchestrating a sophisticated campaign to influence the presidential election in Mexico - the latest smear against Moscow following allegations involving the US presidential vote, the UK Brexit referendum, elections in France and Kenya, and Catalonia's secession vote.

US National Security Adviser H.R. McMaster claims there is evidence of "Russian meddling" in Mexican elections set for July, according to a video obtained by Mexican newspaper Reforma.

Although Russia denies the allegation, the claims illustrate the increasing fears about Russia's use of advanced cyber tools to spread disinformation. The Czech Republic is worried that its own presidential election this week is the next target, the Financial Times reports, while Italy has started working with Facebook to help prevent "fake news" ahead of Italian elections on 4 March.

So has the Kremlin negated the concept of free and fair elections? The Week examines the allegations and looks at possible solutions.

Brexit Referendum

Damian Collins, chair of Britain's Digital, Culture, Media and Sport Select Committee, has given Facebook and Twitter a deadline of 18 January to hand over information about possible Russian misinformation campaigns linked to the 2016 Brexit vote.

"Russian meddling: are free and fair elections impossible?" Dennis Publishing Ltd. Reprinted by permission.

While the UK government insists that Russian propaganda had "no direct successful influence" on the Brexit referendum outcome, a study by the Oxford Internet Institute identified 416 tweets about Brexit published by the Internet Research Agency, a troll farm with ties to the Kremlin. UK researchers do not yet have access to equivalent information from Facebook, "which may be more influential over public opinion than Twitter", The Economist says, and "would almost certainly be part of any sophisticated propaganda operation".

US Presidential Election

Did the Kremlin interfere in the US presidential race? US President Donald Trump and Russian leader Vladimir Putin say no. Many others say yes.

US intelligence agencies claim Putin ordered actions aimed at interfering with the election, including the cybertheft of private data, the placement of propaganda against particular candidates, and general efforts to undermine public faith in the US democratic process, says fact-checking website PolitFact.

Two state-run Russian websites, RT and Sputnik International, acted as "conduits for misinformation", says Newsweek, citing reports in the US intelligence community.

Catalonia's Separation Vote

Spain's struggle with Catalan separatists may have been exacerbated by Russian hackers engaged in a propaganda effort to divide Europe. The Spanish government-backed Elcano Royal Institute, in Madrid, says unidentified Russian "troll" accounts spread inflammatory messages and claims - some true, some false - on social media in the run-up to the 1 October independence referendum.

"Russia has a nationalist agenda, and it supports nationalist, populist movements in Europe because that serves to divide Europe," senior analyst Mira Milosevich told Bloomberg.

According to Spanish newspaper El Pais, an influential tweet about the referendum posted by WikiLeaks founder Julian Assange

- who is still holed up in Equator's London embassy - went viral as a result of activity on fake social media accounts.

Russia dismisses the claims as "hysteria".

French Election

Did RT and Sputnik interfere in the 2017 French presidential election?

Two days before the vote, "hackers leaked nine gigabytes of emails from candidate Emmanuel Macron's campaign onto the web", Wired reports. Although public evidence can't definitively prove Russia's involvement, National Security Agency director Michael Rogers suggested to Congress "that America's most powerful cybersecurity agency has pinned at least some electoral interference on Moscow", the website says.

Kenya's Two Elections

In an interview last September with National Public Radio (NPR), former presidential candidate Hillary Clinton drew comparisons between her election loss and the Kenyan election, which was eventually won by Uhuru Kenyatta after a second vote was held. Kenya's Supreme Court annulled the first vote, after finding the process unfair and lacking in transparency.

Clinton said the US and Kenyan elections were both "a project of Cambridge Analytica", a US-based data company at the centre of a growing controversy over the use of personal information to influence votes. There are problems with Clinton's comparison, however. Concerns about the Kenyan election related to the transmission of the votes, not Cambridge Analytica.

"Still," says The *Washington Post*, "her comments serve to highlight the growing role of large data companies, particularly Cambridge Analytica, in elections well beyond the United States and Europe."

Cyber Solutions?

Halting the flow of misinformation is notoriously difficult, but are there ways to combat the risk of election tampering?

France, Ireland and Germany have all either passed laws or are considering legislation aimed at blocking fabricated social media content.

The Czech Republic, meanwhile, has set up a Centre against Terrorism and Hybrid Threats, an interior ministry unit tasked with combating risks ranging from terrorism to state propaganda, the FT reports. The centre will offer analysis to government departments and target "fake news" - mainly via a Twitter feed - to debunk false stories.

The *Washington Post* argues that the key to strengthening cybersecurity in the US is better communication, more coordination at the individual, group and state levels, and new government regulations "mandating upgrades in cybersecurity for everyone and everything involved in the electoral process". US senators introduced a bill in December to improve and streamline information about cyberthreats between state and federal entities, CBS News reports.

The social media giants may also have a role to play. Facebook turned over more than 3,000 suspicious adverts to the US House Intelligence Committee in October, claiming the ads were purchased by an organisation connected to Russian intelligence services during the 2016 election. Facebook is also planning to label ads as paid content so that it is clear to users who is behind the material, NPR reports.

It remains to be seen, however, whether it is enough to rely on social media to solve a problem that is, at least partly, of their own making.

America's Outrage Over Russian Meddling Is a Double Standard

Damon Linker

Damon Linker is a senior correspondent at TheWeek.com *and a consulting editor at the University of Pennsylvania Press. In recent years, he has taught critical writing at the University of Pennsylvania and worked as a senior editor at* Newsweek/The Daily Beast.

The extent to which the presidential campaign of Donald Trump was aware of (and perhaps even colluded with) the Russian government to interfere with the 2016 election remains uncertain. But that the Russian government *did* interfere with the 2016 election is not.

That became clearer than ever last Friday, when the Justice Department announced the indictment of 13 Russian nationals and three companies, charging them with stealing the identities of American citizens, posing as activists, and working in a multitude of ways to manipulate the outcome of the vote.

But what exactly was the government of Russian President Vladimir Putin attempting to achieve with its meddling? And what is the proper American response?

On these questions, pundits writing from the supposedly sensible ideological center of American politics appear to agree: Putin wanted to elect Trump, and his (shockingly successful) effort may well have constituted an act of war. Some, like foreign policy analyst Max Boot and *New York Times* columnist Tom Friedman, even go so far as to imply that President Trump is a traitor for failing to retaliate — a shirking of responsibility equivalent in its gravity to an imagined George W. Bush shrugging his shoulders in indifference following the 9/11 attack.

Such claims may come from the center, but they are anything but sensible.

Of course we don't want Russia meddling in our elections. And yes, we absolutely should be working to protect ourselves against such interference in the future. But if Putin's mischief-making constituted an act of war against the United States, then the U.S. has committed acts of war against an astonishingly long list of countries since the end of World War II. One study estimates that we interfered with no fewer than 81 elections in 45 nations from 1946 to 2000. Such efforts have been so brazen and uncontroversial that former CIA Director James Woolsey recently felt comfortable laughing about them with Laura Ingraham on Fox News.

This doesn't mean that we should respond to Putin's program of manipulation with indifference. Far from it. But it does mean that a response of self-righteous indignation is risible. To treat such meddling as an act of war on the part of Russia is either to invoke a blatant double standard that permits the U.S. to do things we stridently denounce in others — or it's to admit that our own actions have been far more pernicious than we like to think. We definitely need to protect the integrity of our elections, but we should do so without placing ourselves unconvincingly on the moral high ground.

The second and more serious problem with the "act of war" line is that it grows out of a misperception of what Russia was really trying to accomplish in its meddling. Those who stake out the most strident position on Russian electoral interference often emphasize that Putin wanted Trump to prevail — and that he succeeded, ending up with a Manchurian Candidate in the Oval Office.

Between Clinton and Trump, Putin undoubtedly preferred Trump — among other reasons because he had every reason to expect that a Trump administration would be less geopolitically confrontational than a Clinton one. Yet Putin's aims went far beyond attempting to manipulate the precise outcome of the vote in one way or the other. We know this because of the range of positions that the indicted individuals and companies endorsed in their online interventions. They defended Trump, yes, but they also attacked him, and attacked Clinton, while both championing and denouncing Black Lives Matter, and defending Bernie Sanders and Jill Stein.

The goal wasn't so much to elect one candidate over another. It was to intensify pre-existing polarization in American political culture, thereby provoking chaos as well as (in the words of journalist Julian Sanchez) sowing "doubt about the integrity and fairness of American elections." As I argued in a column nearly a year ago, Putin's calling card isn't the standard totalitarian (communist or fascist) approach of pushing one propagandistic line ("Elect Trump!"). Putin's approach to electoral manipulation is far more postmodern: the effort to inspire confusion, doubt, suspicion, and despair in the electorate about the possibility of ever finding a truth that everyone can affirm.

In an illuminating podcast I quoted in that old column, author Anne Applebaum explained how Putin's government deployed this technique after a mysterious explosion brought down a passenger jet over Ukraine in July 2014. Instead of pushing a single false account of what destroyed the plane, Russia attempted to "pollute the information space" by spreading a huge number of contradictory accounts of what might have happened, some of them plausible, others of them completely fanciful.

Tell a multitude of lies — and stir the pot of ideological disagreement and divisiveness in the country — and eventually people won't know what to believe. And once people have given up trying to tell truth from falsehood, or "my tribe's truth" from truth in itself, a petty dictator can get away with pretty much anything he wants.

That sounds downright dangerous — and it certainly is. But it would be ridiculous to blame Putin for it. Russia undoubtedly contributed (and still contributes) in some small way to the trend, but in the run-up to the election we were doing a remarkably good job of trolling ourselves all on our own. And it's gotten far worse since then — as we see all too clearly every single day on Twitter, and in the highly polarized response to the Russian investigation itself.

Putin pushed us a bit further in the direction we were already headed. That's bad, but not nearly as bad as some would have us believe — and nowhere near as troubling as taking an honest look in the mirror.

Finally, Russia Successfully Interfered in a US Election

Casey Michel

Casey Michel is a reporter for ThinkProgress. *He was formerly a Peace Corps volunteer in Kazakhstan, and he received his master's degree from Columbia University's Harriman Institute.*

For Moscow, the stakes during the US presidential election were crystal-clear. Faced with a candidate who painted the Kremlin as an adversary and obstacle to the spread of liberal democracy, the higher-ups in Moscow decided to do what they could to tilt the vote towards a more welcoming option. As such, over a year before Americans went to the polls, the Kremlin unleashed its efforts. Orders went out to penetrate the staffs of opposing campaigns. Calls went to agents abroad, assessing the possibility of infiltrating the US and spreading rumors about the favored candidate.

But this wasn't 2016—this, rather, was 1984. Cambridge historian Christopher Andrew's 1999 magnum opus on the Mitrokhin Archive—a mountain of documents smuggled out by a former KGB archivist—details how Moscow worked tirelessly, if unsuccessfully, to tip the balance against Ronald Reagan's reelection. As Andrew wrote in his book, *The Sword and the Shield*, the KGB's headquarters "made clear that *any* candidate, of either party, would be preferable to Reagan."

Of course, as Walter Mondale well knows, Moscow's efforts came to naught, with the Kremlin watching its own empire crumble just seven years later. Contrast that, however, with everything we've learned over the past week about Russia's alleged efforts to discredit Hillary Clinton's campaign and America's broader electoral legitimacy. From the outlines shared in the Director of

"Russia has tried to manipulate US elections since the Cold War—so how did they just now succeed?" by Casey Michel, Quartz Media LLC, January 13, 2017. Reprinted by permission.

National Intelligence's recent report—which actually nods to the Mitrokhin Archive as a source—to the stupefying, sordid details of the unverified but explosive dossier on president-elect Donald Trump published this week, it's clear that Moscow had the means, and the mettle, to carve a path for its favorite candidate to the White House. And in 2016, these efforts may have finally paid off.

Yet we must not view the events of 2016 as unprecedented. It's important to keep in mind that Moscow's meddling is not a new phenomenon. And it that sense, while the outcome is still mind-boggling, American politicians and intelligence officials should not be surprised that a foreign antagonist would seek to find a way to tweak and manipulate America's democratic model for its own ends.

Besides the well-documented 1984 campaign, Andrew writes that in 1960, the KGB's Washington agent "was ordered to 'propose diplomatic or propaganda initiatives, or any other measures, to facilitate [John F.] Kennedy's victory.'" (The spy's attempt to make contact with Robert Kennedy, as Andrew noted, "was politely rebuffed.") In 1968, as detailed in the memoir of the Soviet Union's long-serving ambassador to the US, Anatoly Dobrynin, Moscow ordered its man in Washington to offer Democratic candidate Hubert Humphrey "any conceivable help" during the election—including financing the campaign outright. Humphrey eventually lost the race, but he can at least maintain that he refused any Soviet funding.

Then there were the events of 1948, when the Soviet Union threw its support behind third-party candidate and former vice president Henry Wallace. While Wallace's candidacy ended up as little more than a longshot—he failed to land a single vote in the Electoral College—it's not surprising that Moscow pushed his candidacy. This was a man who, as vice president under Franklin Roosevelt, saw both of his preferred candidates for secretary of defense and secretary of state later outed as Soviet agents

Precedent aside, however, manipulating elections has always been part of the spy game—for the United States. As UCLA historian Marc Trachtenberg wrote this week in *Foreign Policy*, "Since 1945, America has intervened in the internal political affairs of other countries as a matter of course." If anything, there's an argument to be made that electoral meddling was one of America's primary Cold War-era tools for managing allies and hot spots alike.

Look, for instance, at recent research from Carnegie Mellon post-doc Dov Levin, whose most recent research on Washington- and Moscow-led meddling offers important context for Cold War-era practices. To wit, as Levin found, the US's most frequent targets for election interference were nominal allies, including Italy and Japan. (Italy, unfortunately, also tied with Finland for the nation in Levin's tally with the greatest number of elections targeted by Moscow, following only West Germany.) Likewise, per Levin's research, Moscow's meddling actually plummeted in the mid-1970s, bottoming out by the time Leonid Brezhnev's gerontocracy passed. And while the US's vote-spinning efforts— as far as historians know, at least—peaked in the early 1950s, Washington also increased its efforts during the 1970s before plateauing under Reagan.

And yet, despite all of this shared history, it appears 2016 may well be the first time in which a foreign power's efforts proved so fruitful. Even if the allegations in the recent Russia-related dossier on Trump prove to be exaggerated or even false, this is still a president-elect who publicly pressed Russia to hack his political rivals. It appears that Moscow's previous attempts had been missing one key ingredient: a candidate willing to take the Kremlin's aid and run with it—all the way to the White House.

Stealing Elections Is Business As Usual

Stephen M. Walt

Stephen M. Walt is a professor of international affairs at Harvard University's John F. Kennedy School of Government. He previously taught at Princeton University and the University of Chicago, where he served as Master of the Social Science Collegiate Division and Deputy Dean of Social Sciences.

Ever since Donald Trump won the presidency last November, perhaps no issue has consumed America's political class more than the question of whether Russia interfered in the U.S. election. The White House, the FBI, and the rest of the intelligence community says it did, although the government has still not provided the public with the concrete evidence on which that conclusion is based. With the legitimacy of his election on the line, Trump has gone from dismissing the allegations entirely (and denigrating the intelligence community) to saying any possible Russian activities had no effect on the outcome. After all, he tweeted, the Russians didn't hack any voting machines, so anything else they may have done is irrelevant.

Lost in the furor over what Moscow did or did not do, and what effects it did or did not have, is the broader question of what this incident says about Russian intentions and aims. Just how unusual was it for great powers to interfere in a democracy's electoral processes, and just how outraged should Americans be by the alleged activities?

Distinguished historian Marc Trachtenberg, professor emeritus at UCLA, thinks all this outrage is naive, and evidence of a clear double standard. In the following guest column, he provides some historical perspective that might temper our collective outrage just a bit. His point is not that Americans should be complacent

"Stealing Elections Is All in the Game," by Stephen M. Walt, Foreign Policy, January 10, 2017. Reprinted by permission.

or unconcerned by these activities, but rather that we should be neither surprised by them nor quick to see them as evidence of newfound Russian hostility. Instead, he suggests, this interference is a type of behavior that the United States helped establish; indeed, meddling in other countries' politics has been an American specialty for a long time.

One might even go a step further: This sort of thing is just "business as usual" in the competitive world of international politics: It's not like states didn't interfere in one another's internal politics in ancient Greece, in the Renaissance, or in the first half of the 20th century. If so, then the real lesson is to fix our own system so that such interventions won't matter, instead of focusing solely on what Putin did or not do.

A Double Standard?

By Marc Trachtenberg

The American political class has been working itself into a lather over the hacking of a number of email accounts affiliated with the Democratic Party, evidently by Russian intelligence, and the subsequent leaking of information from those emails during the recent presidential election campaign. Those leaks, it is said, hurt Hillary Clinton and might well have cost her the election.

The prevailing view is that what the Russians did was intolerable — that what we had here was an outrageous intrusion by a foreign power into our internal democratic political process. You don't hear much nowadays about transparency and the "public's right to know." What is emphasized instead is the threat to American democracy posed by those Russian actions. What nerve the Russians had even trying to hack into the private communications of American political leaders! What nerve they had trying to influence our presidential election!

But isn't there a bit of a double standard at work here? The complainers certainly know that the U.S. government eavesdrops, as a matter of course, on the private communications of many people around the world. The National Security Agency, whose job it is to do this kind of eavesdropping, has a budget of about $10 billion, and, according to an article that came out in the *Washington Post* a few years ago, intercepts and stores "1.7 billion e-mails, phone calls and other types of communications" every day.

The NSA has scored some extraordinary successes over the years. At one point during the Cold War, a recently declassified history of the NSA tells us, a U.S. intercept operation operating out of the American Embassy in Moscow "was collecting and exploiting the private car phone communications of Politburo leaders." As Bob Woodward noted in 1987, "elite CIA and National Security Agency teams," called "Special Collection Elements," could "perform espionage miracles, delivering verbatim transcripts from high-level foreign-government meetings in Europe, the Middle East and Asia, and phone conversations between key politicians." And the U.S. government was not just spying on enemies and terrorists. It was, and presumably still is, very interested in what the leaders of friendly countries are saying to one another. In 1973, for example, Arthur Burns, then chairman of the Federal Reserve Board, noted in his diary that the U.S. government apparently knew "everything that goes on at German cabinet meetings."

Should we be outraged by any of this? This sort of spying, when we do it, is widely accepted. I doubt whether there is a single member of the U.S. national security establishment who would like to go back to the days when "gentlemen did not read each other's mail." But if we're going to eavesdrop on other countries, we shouldn't be too surprised — let alone indignant — when other countries do it to us.

In the present case, however, it is not just the hacking that people object to. It is the fact that this information was used to influence our election. But here, too, a certain double standard is at work. Since 1945, America has intervened in the internal political affairs of other countries as a matter of course. Our basic attitude has been that free elections are great — as long as they don't produce outcomes the U.S. government doesn't like. Many of these episodes — Indochina, Congo, Chile, the Dominican Republic, and so on — are quite well-known. Other cases — like Guyana, where the Kennedy administration put heavy pressure on the British to prevent Cheddi Jagan from coming to power through the democratic process — are less familiar. The practice was more common during the Cold War than people realize.

Indeed, the United States felt free to intervene, sometimes massively, in the internal political affairs of our democratic allies. To be sure, most people are vaguely aware of the fact that such interventions were common in the late 1940s. To cite but one example: The U.S. ambassador in Paris, according to his diary, told the French prime minister in 1947, "no Communists in gov. or else." But even after the situation in Western Europe had stabilized, direct intervention was by no means out of the question if the stakes were high enough. The Eisenhower administration, for example, made it clear to the German people how it wanted them to vote in their 1953 elections; That intervention, according to German political scientists who studied this issue closely, resulted in a landslide victory for the conservative Konrad Adenauer government. A decade later, however, after the Americans had soured on Adenauer, the U.S. government played a leading role in driving him from power — an extraordinary episode that, even today, few people on either side of the Atlantic know much about.

None of this should be dismissed as ancient history. The habits that were formed during the Cold War period remain very much intact. The U.S. government still feels it has the right to influence the outcomes of elections in other countries. Everyone remembers how President Barack Obama warned the British, just before the Brexit vote, that if they chose to leave the European Union, they would be "in the back of the queue" when it came to making trade deals with the United States. Perhaps Obama was just warning British voters about the inevitable consequences and not making an explicit (if subdued) threat; but in either case he was actively trying to influence the outcome of the referendum itself.

But the less well-known case of America's involvement in Ukrainian politics is far more revealing. In 2014, Victoria Nuland, a high State Department official, was taped, presumably by Russian intelligence, talking with the U.S. ambassador in Kiev, Geoffrey Pyatt. The tape of that intercepted phone conversation was soon posted on YouTube. It was clear that Nuland and Pyatt had strong feelings about who should be running things in Ukraine. It was also clear that the United States (to use Pyatt's term) had a "scenario" for bringing about the political changes that were to its liking. As the *Washington Post* put it, they spoke "like political strategists, or perhaps like party bosses in a smoky backroom. Using shorthand and nicknames, they game out what they would like to see opposition figures do and say, and discuss how best to influence some opposition decision-making." None of this was considered out of bounds, and the Nuland affair did not even get much attention at the time. Nuland was certainly not fired from her job. The finger was instead pointed at the Russians for having had the audacity to listen in on and then leak that phone conversation in the first place.

The assumption is that while we have the right to intervene in the internal political affairs of all kinds of countries around the world, it is outrageous if any of them try to do the same thing to us. We have the right to eavesdrop on the private communications of the leaders of foreign countries, but it is outrageous that they should try to hack into the email accounts of American leaders and their associates. America is the "indispensable nation," and the rules that apply to other countries simply do not apply to us. Those are the unspoken assumptions, and it's not hard to imagine how foreigners react to the sort of behavior they lead to. Does the word "arrogant" come to mind here?

My own feeling is that a double standard of this sort is morally repulsive and politically counterproductive. I don't think we should arrogate to ourselves rights that we would not grant to others. But what that means is that, given the way we behave, we should not get too upset if other countries behave the same way. If we approach the recent email hacking affair with those thoughts in mind, we should be able to take what the Russians did in stride. It was in line with the way the world works — a world that is in large part of our own making.

An Open and Fair Government Can Uphold Election Integrity

Alex Howard

Alex Howard is an independent writer and open government advocate based in Washington, DC. He is the founder and operator of the blog e-PluribusUnum.org, *which is a top blog on government information technology. Previously, he was a senior analyst at the Sunlight Foundation and the first senior editor for technology and society at the* Huffington Post.

Here's the good news: The 2016 election is not rigged.

Here's the bad news: Across the United States, the local officials charged with conducting a free and fair election are facing an unprecedented wave of distrust.

"We have never seen this amount of calls. We spend an inordinate amount of time … responding to people," Tom Schedler, secretary of state for Louisiana, said in October at the Bipartisan Policy Center, commenting on rigging claims. "There is no validity to that whatsoever," he said. "Unfortunately, most people we're responding to, it makes no difference what you show them to debunk the theory — they don't believe it."

Unfortunately, public outcry isn't focused on the problems that have led to the U.S. election system being ranked at the bottom of Western democracies by the Election Integrity Project, like gerrymandering, discriminatory electoral laws, campaign finance or voter registration accuracy.

Instead, they're focused on *process*, like polling stations, vote counting and post-election results, all of which the U.S. compares well; research shows that voter fraud is vanishingly rare in the United States, with clerical errors and bad data accounting for most reports. In the face of these bogus voter fraud claims, what can federal, state and local officials do?

Here are four ways for the members of the public and government officials to use transparency and accountability to help mitigate rumors, conspiracy theories and false claims.

Build in Resiliency and Backup Systems

Unfortunately, it's reasonable to expect that the widespread disruptions to internet services in October may have been a preview of what to expect on Election Day.

If voters do not vote early, they should make sure to find their polling place in advance of Tuesday. Take a moment to Google "find my polling place" and print it out.

Election officials would be wise to maintain local databases on mobile devices and print out lists of registered voters in case they lose access to voter registration systems due to online outages.

Newsrooms should shore up security across organizational social media accounts and web servers to protect against compromise and dissemination of false reports. This is particularly true of Associated Press reporters and editors, whose accounts and voting data have become a critical part of Election Day infrastructure.

Publish and Promulgate Explanations of Checks and Balances

States, counties and cities should post clear explanations of the electoral process on websites, push them out on social media and accept media requests to discuss how the voting process works. Ideally, these will go beyond an outline of the voting process, as provided by the Massachusetts Secretary of the Commonwealth's Office, to explain how state laws anticipate human errors and build in safeguards to address them.

They'll point out that polling places are public spaces, at libraries or schools, and community centers open to the public, like churches or gyms. They'll describe how the ballots and voting machine are kept secure prior to voting, with seals that show tampering, and that observers can check them. They'll explain how political parties and campaigns can send watchers to observe the safety and integrity of Election Day, and how lawful poll watchers are trained. They'll lay out how election officials keep records of who voted and how. They'll explain and document how every step of the electoral process works, including ballot preparation, testing of equipment, voting early, by absentee and on Election Day, and the count, transmission and certification of results. They'll provide every possible reason for voters to trust that they have verified the integrity of the election.

There *will* be lines, errors, mistakes, misconfigurations, conflicts and other problems on Election Day. Transparency and accountability about what happened and what was done are democracy's best protectors.

Report Problems to Electionland and the FBI

Voter intimidation is illegal. Certified poll watchers are there to protect you and your right to vote, *not* to prevent you from voting or discourage you. If you experience extreme or abusive intimidation at the polls, call 911 and contact the local law enforcement present. You should also report all instances of voter intimidation to the FBI Civil Rights Division: Staff at 1-800-253-3931. You can also voice complaints, problems or concerns related to voting by fax 202-307-3961, by email to voting.section@usdoj.gov and by complaint forms that may be submitted here.

If you aren't subject to voter intimidation — and we hope you aren't! — please consider sharing your experience at the polls with Electionland, a nationwide collaboration of nonprofit media outlets that are documenting the 2016 election. Text "ELECTIONLAND" to 69866 to participate, or submit a report online.

Stand Up and Decry Misinformation

It's not enough for federal officials, members of Congress or the White House to stand up for the integrity of the elections, particularly in a moment of extreme partisan polarization. It's incumbent on state and local officials, particularly secretaries of state, to explain to voters how elections are conducted. Given unprecedented concerns about foreign actors seeking to influence elections, it's also critical for officials to explain how electronic voting systems are secured and protected.

A recent panel on election integrity at the Aspen Institute featured Edgardo Cortés, commissioner of the Virginia Department of Elections, describing both the security provisions that their systems follow, like an "airgap" from the internet, and the checks and balances present at each polling station, from observers to counts in public, and following the vote, in the certification process. Common Cause's steps to secure our election are a useful outline as well.

On Election Day, remember that other nations may have an interest in undermining trust in our election. As with wars and natural disaster, pranksters will be online. Beware videos and doctored images from previous years or other locations.

Don't spread rumors and conspiracies using your own social media accounts. Read the Verification Handbook. Google claims first, search for the link on Twitter, consult Snopes.com to see if it's a debunked rumor, consider the authority of the publication (beware fake news sites!) and then decide whether to share the story. Please *do* share verified fact-checks of rumors: They change minds.

We hope that you'll turn out to vote! Go find your polling place and exercise your most fundamental democratic right.

The Blame for Interference in the 2016 Election Falls on Many Heads

Philip Ewing

Philip Ewing is NPR's national security editor. He helps direct coverage of the military, the intelligence community, counterterrorism, veterans, and other topics for the radio and online.

Why didn't then-President Barack Obama stop Russia's campaign of active measures against the 2016 presidential campaign?

President Trump has been casting blame on his predecessor for not acting against the scheme since Justice Department special counsel Robert Mueller brought indictments against a batch of Russians and Russian entities on Friday for the role they played.

FACT CHECK

This story is complex and goes beyond a simple "True" or "False" grade. One basic notion that is false is the idea the Obama administration took no action — it did. The question that has been asked many times since the presidential election is why it didn't do more.

Private Warnings

Among other things, top U.S. intelligence officials — including then-CIA Director John Brennan — privately warned their Russian counterparts not to persist with their active measures. Obama himself told Russian President Vladimir Putin not to interfere in the election. These warnings did not work.

Publicity

Obama administration officials also told reporters on background that Russian intelligence operatives were behind the cyberattacks that led to the release of emails stolen from political figures and institutions. Later, Director of National Intelligence James Clapper and Homeland Security Secretary Jeh Johnson formally blamed the Russian government in an official statement.

Although it wasn't universally accepted, the active measures campaign became a part of the political campaign itself. Trump and opponent Hillary Clinton traded barbs about the Russian interference during their debates.

Trump has gone back and forth about what he accepts and what he doesn't about the nature of the attack. Sometimes he acknowledges it; other times he has cited the denials he has gotten from Putin, saying, "I really believe that when he tells me that, he means it."

The president's position since Friday's indictments has been that the interference campaign did take place — but that he and his campaign had nothing to do with it. On that point, Trump has been consistent: There was, he says, "no collusion."

Mueller is focused on whether that is so and whether Trump may have broken the law if he tried to frustrate the investigation. More on this below.

Diplomatic Response

After Election Day, Obama ordered the U.S. intelligence community to issue a public report about the Russian scheme. Once it had — and concluded Russia's attack was aimed at helping Trump and hurting Clinton — the United States imposed a slate of punitive measures against Moscow. In addition to imposing new sanctions, Washington also expelled a number of Russian diplomats and closed two Russian diplomatic compounds in Maryland and New York.

So Why Didn't Obama's Administration Do More?

That isn't clear. Some former administration officials who have talked about it publicly have reproached themselves for not acting more aggressively. There also was a long-standing criticism of Obama that his foreign-policy making amounted to endless process with no outcomes — hours of meetings that yielded more meetings but no ultimate action.

Plus, the relationship between the United States and Russia is multifaceted and often intensely complicated:

- Obama scaled back missile defense plans in Europe to placate Moscow.
- Obama wanted Russia to play a role in the international agreement under which Iran agreed to restrict its nuclear program — and Putin went along.
- Obama spent the end of his presidency trying to bring Russia into a multilateral agreement to end the Syrian civil war, but Foreign Minister Sergey Lavrov ultimately never committed.

So Obama's team had to manage many spinning plates in addition to the active measures campaign it detected by the middle of 2016. One question Obama may address in his book is why he calibrated his choices in the way he did — whether he looked the other way on election interference to keep open other options elsewhere.

A Partisan Tightrope

Former Vice President Joe Biden also has complained that the White House wanted Republicans to join in a bipartisan statement announcing and condemning the interference campaign. In Biden's telling, however, Senate Majority Leader Mitch McConnell, R-Ky., wouldn't go along.

But that didn't stop then-Senate Minority Leader Harry Reid, D-Nev., from alluding publicly to the Russian campaign in a letter to then-FBI Director James Comey. And Comey reportedly wanted to announce the active measures in an op-ed column, as Newsweek reported in March 2017. Two sources with knowledge about the matter told *Newsweek* that Obama administration officials blocked the effort.

There's no way to know what difference it might have made for U.S. officials to have confirmed and condemned the Russian interference in real time.

Obama administration officials have said they worried about appearing to put their thumb on the scales for Clinton. Combined with Obama's belief that Clinton would win, their political calculus appears to have boiled down to: Let's ride this out.

Obama himself said in December 2016 that he wasn't convinced that he should have done anything different.

"There have been folks out there who suggest somehow if we went out there and made big announcements and thumped our chests about a bunch of stuff, that somehow it would potentially spook the Russians," he said. "I think it doesn't read the thought process in Russia very well."

FACT CHECK

The intelligence community did not make an assessment about how the active measures campaign affected the 2016 election. Trump and supporters have sometimes said incorrectly that the report found there was no effect; in fact, it did not address the question. Homeland Security officials did conclude that cyberattacks didn't tamper with vote tallies in 2016.

Why Aren't Democrats Under Investigation?

Some of them may be. FBI special agents in Arkansas are reportedly conducting an investigation into the Clinton Foundation. But Trump and his allies, especially Republicans in the House, want more. They say this story is about abuse of power by the FBI and Justice Department and "bias" within those agencies against the president.

Trump wants Attorney General Jeff Sessions to do more work to expose those aspects of the story. He may, but so far Sessions and Deputy Attorney General Rod Rosenstein have said they don't see enough cause to appoint a second special counsel in addition to Mueller.

Why Is Trump Under Investigation?

Part of Russia's active measures campaign included clandestine overtures from human intelligence operatives to people in the Trump campaign. When the FBI learned that a junior foreign policy adviser in London got offers of "dirt" on Clinton or "off the record" meetings with top Russian officials, it began a counterintelligence investigation that continues to this day.

Several other people in the Trump campaign had contacts with Russians before and after Election Day. Trump's son Donald Trump Jr. received an email that included what was described as an offer of help for the campaign from the Russian government.

"If it's what you say, I love it," Trump Jr. wrote back.

He later hosted a delegation that included a Russian attorney and a Russian-American lobbyist; the details of what took place in the meeting are disputed.

More contacts took place. An adviser traveled to Moscow. Other contacts involved Sessions — then an Alabama senator, who now serves as attorney general but is lately the target of Trump's ire — and Jared Kushner, Trump's son-in-law, who today is dueling behind the scenes with White House chief of staff John Kelly.

The contacts continued until just before the inauguration. As Obama was imposing punitive measures against Moscow following the election, Trump's administration-in-waiting was asking its Russian interlocutors not to retaliate.

Retired Lt. Gen. Mike Flynn, Trump's national security adviser, asked Russia's then-ambassador to the U.S. to hold off because it could expect a different approach once Trump was inaugurated. Putin agreed.

There have also been suggestions that Flynn and the Trump administration planned not only to renegotiate financial restrictions with Moscow once Trump was in office but had already decided before the fact to lift sanctions.

Flynn has pleaded guilty to lying to the FBI about the conversations he had with Russia's ambassador and is cooperating with Mueller's investigation.

The Foreign Agents Registration Act and How It Can Combat Interference

Melissa Yeager

Melissa Yeager has worked as a senior staff writer for the Sunlight Foundation and is a Robert Bosch fellow.

Before his resignation on Friday, news stories and questions have swirled about Donald Trump's former campaign manager Paul Manafort and his involvement with pro-Russian politicians in Ukraine. What was his role? Was he paid? Who does he have ties to? Was he disclosing what he needed to under U.S. law?

Given the renewed attention to the role influence from foreign governments has allegedly had on this year's presidential election cycle, you may have heard pundits talk about FARA, or the Foreign Agents Registration Act. There's likely to be more debate in the coming weeks about who should have and who did register with FARA.

So, what the heck is FARA?! Glad you asked.

In 1938, Congress passed the Foreign Agents Registration Act, which requires those working on behalf of a foreign government or a quasi-government agency to disclose information about their activities. Congress passed the act as a response to the Nazi propaganda that was entering the United States during World War II, and was supposed to give members of Congress and the American people more knowledge about foreign interests trying to influence U.S. politics.

A lot of people compare it to lobbying disclosure, but that may not be an "apples to apples" comparison as it includes many other "influence" activities, like public relations and tourism. Congress believed that if you were a foreign actor in the U.S., your disclosure should be deeper and broader; this was not just a lobbying disclosure act, but a counter-espionage provision of the law meant to provide transparency to areas of potential foreign influence.

FARA requires that someone register with the Department of Justice within 10 days of agreeing to be an agent. Then that individual must file reports every six months detailing their activities.

Some of the things they have to disclose:

- The name of the foreign government
- Whom they have contacted, including government officials, members of Congress, their staff and also members of the media
- What issues they discussed
- How much money they received for that activity
- Copies of any informational items (formerly called propaganda) distributed; this can include posters, press releases, ads, op-eds and more
- Any campaign contributions made by the registered individual

Some of unique parts of FARA compared to the Lobbying Disclosure Act:

- There is no monetary threshold to FARA, so an agent must register even if that person isn't paid at all
- FARA office collects fees for registering
- FARA makes reports to Congress every six months
- The FARA office can make on-site inspections of records of those registered under the act

While we can glean a lot of information from these reports, it's important to know there are several categories of people exempted as well. Those include:

- Diplomats and officials of foreign governments and their staffs (if recognized by the State Department)
- Activities purely commercial in nature
- Activities that are related to religious, scholastic, academic, scientific or the fine arts

- Sometimes collecting funds used for medical aid, food or clothing to relieve human suffering
- Lawyers representing foreign principals in court so long as they are not influencing policy
- Agents registered under the Lobbying Disclosure Act

Second, the documents are only as good as the integrity of the person filling them out. Sometimes those are handwritten or incomplete. Sometimes people don't register at all.

The Department of Justice provides the filings online, but they are in PDF format and thus are not easy to sort or search. That's why from 2008 to 2013, the Sunlight Foundation undertook a project designed to make those easier to access. Though you can see archived information online — like a feed of arm sales and new registrants — there is still a lot of information that's only available physically at the office, primarily the informational items. Sunlight would love to see this information stored in a machine readable format and available to users online.

Enforcing FARA

The Department of Justice has several avenues of enforcement. The statute has both civil and criminal prosecution avenues. When the FARA Unit discovers potential violations of the act, it first sends a letter of inquiry to the individual seeking more information. But, the Department of Justice lacks authority to inspect the records of those whom they believe should be registered, but haven't. They only have the authority to perform site inspections if the person has already registered under the law.

A 2008 Government Accountability Office report pointed out that congressional action was needed to give the Justice Department this authority. The agency also pointed this out in a 2015 reply to an inquiry by Sen. Grassley, R-Iowa, regarding enforcement of FARA. Grassley's office made the inquiry following news stories questioning the activities of Clinton ally Sidney Blumenthal.

The agency expressed interest in working with Congress to change the part of the law restricting them from inspecting the records of those who had not registered under FARA. Sunlight supports this change, but so far, that has not happened.

But we did get an idea of what the Justice Department has done in terms of enforcement of the law. One of the challenges of FARA is that the Justice Department has to show "willful" violation of the law. It can sometimes be hard to prove that someone intentionally broke the law; individuals can claim they weren't aware of FARA rules in the first place.

When responding to Grassley last year, the Justice Department reported that in the past 10 years:

- It has sent 130 letters of inquiry
- Of those letters sent, the department found 38 had obligation to registered under FARA
- The FARA Unit has conducted 101 inspections since 2005
- FARA has charged four criminal cases

The most recent criminal prosecution happened in 2014. Prince Asiel Ben Israel received a seven month prison sentence after he pleaded guilty to not reporting his activity while trying to persuade U.S. government officials to lift sanctions on Zimbabwean government officials.

The Justice Department's FARA office also told Grassley that the agency finds leads for investigations by reading reports in media outlets — as is the case with Manafort's involvement in Ukraine. We reached out to the Justice Department to ask if it is investigating the situation involving Manafort. Spokesman Marc Raimondi told us by email, "While we would never discuss a specific case beyond what is available on the public FARA website, in general FARA does not authorize the government to inspect records of those not registered under the Act."

In response to our questions, Raimondi also told us, "The Department is considering legislation that would remedy the government's current inability to compel the production of records from potential and current registrants."

But there may be more clarity on FARA's future soon. As Demand Progress' Daniel Schuman pointed out, a report from the Justice Department's inspector general due to come out in the next couple months will examine "the administration and enforcement of" FARA in depth. This report could potentially bring about positive changes in the law regarding data quality, oversight capabilities and more.

Regardless of Manafort's situation and the law's potential limitations, FARA is a key tool for monitoring the ways foreign entities influence policy and opinions in the United States. If you'd like to dig into FARA data yourself, check out Sunlight's Foreign Influence Explorer. And for even more ways to explore FARA, check out the excellent Foreign Influence Database from our allies at the Project on Government Oversight!

Organizations to Contact

The editors have compiled the following list of organizations concerned with the issues debated in this book. The descriptions are derived from materials provided by the organizations. All have publications or information available for interested readers. This list was compiled on the date of publication of the present volume; the information provided here may change. Be aware that many organizations take several weeks or longer to respond to inquiries, so allow as much time as possible.

American Civil Liberty Union (ACLU)
125 Broad Street, 18th Floor
New York NY 10004
phone: (212) 549-2500
email: aclupreferences@aclu.org
website: www.aclu.org

For almost 100 years, the ACLU has worked to defend and preserve the individual rights and liberties guaranteed by the Constitution and laws of the United States.

Brennan Center for Justice
New York University
161 Avenue of the Americas, 12th floor
New York, NY 10013
phone: (626) 292-8310
email: brennancenter@nyu.edu
website: brennancenter.org

The Brennan Center is a nonpartisan law and policy institute at New York University that seeks to improve our systems of democracy and justice. Its work ranges from voting rights to campaign finance reform, from racial justice in criminal law to Constitutional protection in the fight against terrorism.

Campaign Legal Center
1411 K St. NW, Suite 1400
Washington, DC 20005
phone: (202) 736-2200
website: campaignlegalcenter.org

The Campaign Legal Center is a nonpartisan, nonprofit organization that protects and strengthens our democracy in the areas of campaign finance, voting rights, political communication, and government ethics.

Common Cause
1133 19th Street NW, 9th Floor
Washington, DC 20036
phone: (202) 833-1200
email: CauseNet@commoncause.org
website: commoncause.org

Common Cause is a nonpartisan citizens advocacy group that is fighting to ensure that every adult American has easy access to the ballot and that every vote is counted as cast. It works to strengthen laws that protect voting rights, make voting systems secure, reliable, and verifiable, and ensure that every voter has an equal say in elections.

Common Sense Media
650 Townsend, Suite 435
San Francisco, CA 94103
phone: (415) 863-0600
website: www.commonsensemedia.org

Common Sense is the leading independent nonprofit organization dedicated to helping young people thrive in a world of media and technology.

Demos
220 Fifth Ave,. 2nd Fl.
New York, NY 10001
phone: (212) 633-1405
website: demos.org

Demos means "the People." It is a public policy organization working for an America where everyone has an equal say in democracy and an equal chance in the economy. It has nine specialist and experts working on Voting Rights and Voter Registration.

The Fair Elections Legal Network (FELN)
1825 K St. NW Suite 450
Washington DC 20006
phone: (202) 331-0114
email: info@fairelectionsnetwork.com
website: http://fairelectionsnetwork.com

The Fair Elections Legal Network (FELN) is a national, nonpartisan organization focused on voting rights, legal support, and election reform whose mission is to remove barriers to registration and voting for traditionally underrepresented constituencies. FELN works to improve overall election administration through administrative, legal, and legislative reform as well as through providing legal and technical assistance to voter mobilization organizations.

FairVote
6930 Carroll Avenue, Suite 610
Takoma Park, MD 20912
phone: (301) 270-4616
email: info@fairvote.org
website: fairvote.org

FairVote seeks to make representative democracy fair, functional, and representative by developing the analytical and educational tools necessary for its reform partners to secure and sustain improvements to American elections.

Hip Hop Caucus

1638 R Street, NW #120
Washington, DC 20009
phone: (202) 293-5902
email: media@hiphopcaucus.org
website: http://hiphopcaucus.org/

Hip Hop Caucus is empowering communities who are impacted first and worst by injustice.

The League of Women Voters of the United States

1730 M Street NW, Suite 1000
Washington, DC 20036-4508
phone: (202) 429-1965
website:www.lwv.org

The League of Women Voters of the United States encourages informed and active participation in government, works to increase understanding of major public policy issues, and influences public policy through education and advocacy.

MediaSmarts

205 Catherine Street, Suite 100
Ottawa, ON
Canada
K2P 1C3
phone: (613) 224-7721
email: info@mediasmarts.ca
website: mediasmarts.ca

MediaSmarts is a Canadian not-for-profit charitable organization for digital and media literacy.

National Election Defense Coalition

email: info@electiondefense.org
website: www.electiondefense.org

The NEDC is a national network of recognized experts in cybersecurity and elections administration, bipartisan policymakers, and concerned citizens and movement-builders. They are working to build a bipartisan consensus on the need for reform while building a comprehensive, cost-effective plan to secure the vote in coming elections.

Rock the Vote

875 Connecticut Ave NW, 10th Floor
Washington, DC 20009
phone: (202) 719-9910
email: media@rockthevote.org
website: www.rockthevote.org

Rock the Vote is a nonpartisan, nonprofit organization dedicated to building the political power of young people. For over twenty-five years, Rock the Vote has revolutionized the way we use pop culture, music, art, and technology to engage young people in politics and build our collective power.

The United State Elections Project

223 Anderson Hall
PO Box 117325
Gainesville, FL 32611
phone: (352) 273-2371
email: michael.mcdonald@ufl.edu
website: electproject.org

The United State Elections Project's mission is to provide timely and accurate election statistics, electoral laws, research reports, and other useful information regarding the United States' electoral system. By providing this information, the project seeks to inform the people of the United States on how their electoral system works, how it may be improved, and how they can participate in it.

The United States Student Association
PO Box 33486
Washington, DC 20036
email: ops@usstudents.org
website: http://usstudents.org

The United States Student Association is the country's oldest, largest, and most inclusive national student-led organization. It develops current and future leaders and amplifies the student voice at the local, state, and national levels by mobilizing grassroots power to win concrete victories on student issues.

The Voting Rights Alliance
phone: (202) 602 7080
email: barnwine@tjcoalition.org
website: www.votingrightsalliance.net

The Voting Rights Alliance is a growing network of organizations, activists, and legislators working to restore and protect voting rights from concerted attacks that undermine our access to the polls, and to have our votes fairly counted.

Voto Latino
PO Box 35608
Washington DC 20033
phone: (202) 386-6374
email: info@votolatino.org
website: http://votolatino.org

Voto Latino is a pioneering civic media organization that seeks to transform America by recognizing Latinos' innate leadership. Through innovative digital campaigns, pop culture, and grassroots voices, they provide culturally relevant programs that engage, educate, and empower Latinos to be agents of change.

Bibliography

Books

Stacey Abrams. *Minority Leader: How to Lead from the Outside and Make Real Change,* New York, NY: Henry Holt and Company, 2018.

Jules Archer. *Winners and Losers: How Elections Work in America,* New York, NY: Skyhorse Publishing, Inc., 2016

Sarah Armstrong. *Voter Fraud,* New York, NY: Greenhaven Press, 2015.

Ari Berman. *Give Us the Ballot: The Modern Struggle for Voting Rights in America,* New York, NY: Picador, 2016.

Nic Cheesema and Brian Klaas. *How to Rig an Election,* New Haven, CT: Yale University Press, 2018.

Nicholas Croce. *Anarchism, Revolution, and Terrorism,* New York, NY: Britannica Educational Publishing, 2014.

Brian Duignan. *Political Parties, Interest Groups, and Elections,* New York, NY: Britannica Educational Publishing, 2012.

Jeff Fleischer. *Votes of Confidence: A Young Person's Guide to American Elections,* San Francisco, CA: Zest Books, 2016.

Ann Hosein. *Political Science,* New York, NY: Britannica Educational Publishing, 2015.

Dan Pfeiffer. *Yes We (Still) Can: Politics in the Age of Obama, Twitter, and Trump,* New York, NY: Grand Central Publishing, 2018.

Zachary Roth. *The Great Suppression: Voting Rights, Corporate Cash, and the Conservative Assault on Democracy,* New York, NY: Crown, 2016.

Michael Waldman. *The Fight to Vote,* New York, NY: Simon and Schuster, 2016.

Periodicals and Internet Sources

"2016 Presidential Campaign Hacking Fast Facts," *CNN*, May 16, 2018. https://www.cnn.com/2016/12/26/us/2016-presidential-campaign-hacking-fast-facts/index.html.

"Obama vows 'action' against Russia over election hacks," *Times of Israel,* December 16, 2017. https://www.timesofisrael.com/obama-vows-to-take-action-against-russia-over-election-hacks/

"Putin Targets Navalny, Defends Trump, Sets Stage For Reelection With Hours-Long Press Conference," *Radio Free Europe/Radio Liberty*, December 14, 2017. https://www.rferl.org/a/stage-set-putin-final-year-end-press-conference-before-march-presidential-election/28917278.html.

Rachel Ansley, "A Plan to Thwart Russian Meddling," Atlantic Council, February 6, 2018. http://www.atlanticcouncil.org/blogs/new-atlanticist/a-plan-to-thwart-russian-meddling.

Jenni Bergal. "Russian Hacking Fuels Return to Paper Ballots," The Pew Charitable Trust, October 3, 2017. http://www.pewtrusts.org/en/research-and-analysis/blogs/stateline/2017/10/03/russian-hacking-fuels-return-to-paper-ballots.

Robert D. Blackwill and Philip H. Gordon, "Containing Russia, Again: An Adversary Attacked the United States—It's Time to Respond," *Foreign Affairs*, January 19, 2018. https://www.cfr.org/article/containing-russia-again-adversary-attacked-united-states-its-time-respond.

Philip Bump, "What Obama did, didn't do and couldn't do in response to Russian interference," *Washington Post*, February 21, 2017. https://www.washingtonpost.com/news/politics/wp/2018/02/21/what-obama-did-didnt-do-and-couldnt-do-in-response-to-russian-interference/.

Morgan Chalfant, "Senators introduce election security amendment to defense bill," the *Hill*, June 8, 2018. http://

thehill.com/policy/cybersecurity/391380-senators-introduce-election-security-amendment-to-defense-bill.

Adrian Chen, "The Agency" *New York Times Magazine*, June 2, 2015, https://www.nytimes.com/2015/06/07/magazine/the-agency.html.

Kush Desai, "FACT CHECK: Did Obama Know About Russian Meddling And Do 'NOTHING'?" *Check Your Fact*, June 28, 2017. http://checkyourfact.com/2017/06/28/fact-check-did-obama-know-about-russian-meddling-and-do-nothing/.

Zachary Fryer-Biggs, "Meet the new high-tech solution to Russian election hacking: paper ballots," *Vox*, April 3, 2018. https://www.vox.com/2018/4/3/17189906/russian-election-hacking-paper-ballots.

Livia Gershon, "Just How Divided Are Americans Since Trump's Election?" *History Channel*, November 8, 2017, https://www.history.com/news/just-how-divided-are-americans-since-trumps-election.

Dan Gillmor, "The Case for Standardized and Secure Voting Technology," *Atlantic*, May 26, 2017. https://www.theatlantic.com/technology/archive/2017/05/the-case-for-standardized-and-secure-voting-technology/523878/.

Fiona Hill, "3 reasons Russia's Vladimir Putin might want to interfere in the U.S. presidential elections," Brookings, August 3, 2016. https://www.brookings.edu/blog/order-from-chaos/2016/08/03/3-reasons-russias-vladimir-putin-might-want-to-interfere-in-the-u-s-presidential-elections/.

Mathew Ingram, "Mark Zuckerberg Is Starting to Take Some Responsibility for Facebook's Influence," *Fortune*, February 17, 2017. http://fortune.com/2017/02/17/mark-zuckerberg-manifesto-facebook/.

Joshua Keating, "Election Meddling Is Surprisingly Common," *Slate*, January 4, 2017. http://www.slate.com/blogs/the_

slatest/2017/01/04/u_s_and_russian_election_meddling_is_
surprisingly_common.html.

Brendan Nyhan, "Fake News and Bots May Be Worrisome,
but Their Political Power Is Overblown," *New York Times*,
February 13, 2018, https://www.nytimes.com/2018/02/13/
upshot/fake-news-and-bots-may-be-worrisome-but-their-
political-power-is-overblown.html.

Peter Overby, "Federal Election Commission Can't Decide If
Russian Interference Violated Law," *NPR*, May 25, 2018.
https://www.npr.org/2018/05/25/613748826/federal-
election-commission-cant-decide-if-russian-interference-
violated-law.

Joshua Philipp, "Obama's Handling of Russian Election
Interference Meets With Scrutiny," *Epoch Times*, June
28, 2017. https://www.theepochtimes.com/with-russia-
investigations-ongoing-questions-arise-of-why-obama-
didnt-take-action_2262444.html.

Andrea Römmele and Rafael Goldzweig, "Social media can
be a healthier and more democratic space for politics,"
Herite School of Governance, November 15, 2017. https://
www.hertie-school.org/en/debate/folder/social-media-
democracy/.

Alexander Smith, "Putin on U.S. election interference: 'I
couldn't care less,'" *NBC News*, March 9, 2018. https://www.
nbcnews.com/news/world/putin-u-s-election-interference-
i-couldn-t-care-less-n855151.

Shaun Walker, "The Russian troll factory at the heart of the
meddling allegations," *Guardian*, April 2, 2015, https://www.
theguardian.com/world/2015/apr/02/putin-kremlin-inside-
russian-troll-house.

Index